This

Sandra Lee semi-homemade®

gatherings

book belongs to:

....

Meredith® Books Des Moines, Iowa

Library of Congress Control Number 2006930037 ISBN-13: 978-0-696-23437-8 ISBN-10: 0-696-23437-8

198 Chicken Caesar Pizza Salad

82 Lemon-Herb Butter-Basted Chicken

102 Black Jack Lamb Rack

236 Red Velvet Bars

128 Burgandy Bubbler

sem•i-home•made

adj. **1:** a stress-free, solution-based formula that provides savvy shortcuts and affordable, timesaving tips for overextended do-it-yourself homemakers **2:** a quick and easy equation wherein 70% ready-made convenience products are added to 30% fresh ingredients with creative personal style, allowing homemakers to take 100% of the credit for something that looks, feels, or tastes homemade **3:** a foolproof resource for having it all—and having the time to enjoy it **4:** a method created by Sandra Lee for home, garden, crafts, beauty, food, fashion, and entertaining wherein everything looks, tastes, or feels as if it was made from scratch

Solution-based **E**nterprise that **M**otivates, **I**nspires, and **H**elps **O**rganize and **M**anage time, while **E**nriching **M**odern life by **A**dding **D**ependable shortcuts **E**very day.

dedication

To my Aunt Peggy Jo
who makes her home a great place
for us all to gather year-round.

special thanks

To my incredible television production team:
Andy, Carol, Meghan, Craig, Danielle, Dave, Deniz, Ed, Fern,
Guy, Jeff, Jeffrey, Jessica, Jon, Lia, Mark, Matt, Mori, Paul, Rich, Robert,
Ryan, Santos, Stephen, Tom, Susan, Bob, Brooke, Irene, Warren,
Scott, Bryce, Stephanie, Kim

great gratitude

To my year-round publishing family and creative team:
Jack, Bob, Doug, Jim, Jan, Ken, Jeff, Mick, Vicki, Jerry, Cheryl,
Wini, Carrie, Pamela, Mark, Laurent, Gad, Michael, and Savina
Thanks also to:
American Greetings, Feizy Rugs, Fidalgo's, F. Schumacher,
HELP USA (go to helpusa.org/comfortfoods), Snap-On, Waverly Fabrics

Letter from Sandra

The icing on the cake for me is this book, but I must admit its frosting was spread decades ago, baked up in birthday cakes made by my Grandma Lorraine. Whenever my sister Cynthia and I had a birthday, she would bake a single-layer 8" cake for each of us and decorate it with the most amazing things—colored icings, bits of candy, and confetti sprinkles. Then she would take a shiny new aluminum pie pan, turn it upside down to make a pedestal, and serve us our very own child-size cake, decorated with all the things we liked best. Sitting on that silver pie tin, that cake was the height of elegance and proof of the complete adoration of my grandmother.

Cindy (on the left) and I celebrate our birthdays at grandma's. I'm trying my hand at folding a perfect napkin to match our cakes.

This simple act of love taught me a lesson that became the cornerstone of my life and, later, my business—it doesn't matter how much things cost; it matters how exceptional you make someone feel. Love doesn't have a price tag; it's measured in smiles and minutes and bites of cake.

From my Grandma Lorraine, I inherited a love of making things "nice"—choosing just the right foods and colors and decorations to make a table special, without spending a lot to do it. Whether you're hosting a party, celebrating a holiday, or sitting down to dinner with family and friends, beautiful food served on a beautiful table makes a meal memorable. Semi-Homemade® makes it possible. Start with 70% ready-made, store-bought foods, add 30% fresh ingredients, a pinch of creativity, a scoop of fun, and voila—you have scrumptious dishes and easy tablescapes that leave a lasting impression.

Everything you'll see in this book is available at supermarkets, craft stores, or in your own cabinets. I'll help you look at everyday things with a fresh, creative eye. Fruits, desserts, or a bowl of punch become centerpieces. Flowers are picked from the garden or grabbed at the grocery. Napkins are clipped with clothespins; vases fill with shells; place cards sprout from pots. Instead of expensive linens and china, you'll find fabric remnants, mismatched dinnerware, thrift store candlesticks. If you have it, use it, and if you don't—make do with something else. It'll be just as fabulous.

Every day is an occasion to celebrate the company of family and friends—and special days like holidays and birthdays are a chance to show off your heart's fanciful flair. Some are sweet, some are sophisticated, but all are special. That's what this book is all about: Making special people feel special. That's the icing from my grandma's cake—a gift now for you too. So open your home, your heart, and your table to others, because you can have your cake and eat it too. That's the beauty of a Semi-Homemaker®. I wish you everything wonderful.

Cheers to a happy, healthy home, and heart!

Sandra Lee

Table of Contents

Every Day

Special Days

Holidays

112

120

130

136

142

150

158

162

168

174

180

Birthdays

184

188

194

200

Family Days

Tablescapes

Every meal can be a memorable one with just a little attention to detail. Here you'll find interesting, thoughtful, easy-to-create ideas that everyone will admire and appreciate. Best of all, you get to have fun and take all the credit!

Theme: Tablescapes set the mood of each meal whether formal or informal. A formal occasion may mean a more traditional approach to your table, informal means anything can go. But in both cases, you will want to mix and match items such as fabrics, plates, candles, and floral scenes in varying heights, colors, and textures to create interest and drama.

Menu: Simple servings are best. Think pasta, cheeses, and fine wines or something a bit more daring like Wild Teriyaki Wings and Shimmer-tinis. Making smart menus easy is what matters most—think starters (appetizers or salad), main courses, side dishes, desserts, and "cocktail time."

Table Covering: Table coverings are the foundation for your tablescape. By layering coverings it's easy to achieve a finished, refined effect. Establish your table with a base tablecloth (length of fabric) and add an overlay of a decorative fabric to enhance the look. Utilize fabrics off the bolt to gain the greatest selection. Remember, with pinking shears you won't have to sew a stitch.

Centerpiece: Ideas for simple centerpieces flow naturally from the theme. Use fresh or faux flowers and greens with candles on your table whenever possible. For a fun, festive look, use things from around your home. Be creative—think decorative cookie jars, candle collages, teapot collections, even a cluster of miniature birdhouses. Whatever strikes your fancy will work. Display your centerpiece collection on multitiered levels using clear glass cake pedestals, bowls turned upside down, and assorted candlestick holders. These items create varying height platforms to showcase individual centerpiece elements.

Place Cards and Favors: It's fun and easy to create place cards and favors—and even more interesting when they are combined as one tabletop element. Neither needs to be elaborate or expensive; a little ingenuity goes a long way. Think of your guests' interests and likes—sweet treats in themed containers, snapshots in interesting frames, and trinkets in reusable boxes—a gift in a gift is always popular.

Fashion: Match your outfit to your theme. By wearing clothing that matches the color and personality of your table you'll look and feel fabulously fashionable. Food is fashion—so have fun!

Every Day

As children, we love to entertain our friends. We call it a "play date." No special occasion required—simply a sunny day out or a rainy day in is reason enough to invite our friends, real and imaginary, to tea. We arrange cups and saucers just so, share foods we love, and pick flowers from the garden to make our table bloom with life.

Whether we're 6 or 60, the idea is the same: sharing food and fun with those whose company enriches our life. This chapter is filled with inspired pairings—ready-in-minutes recipes and creative tablescapes that bring food and friends together. Your friends make it fun; Semi-Homemade® makes it simple. Say goodbye to days spent planning a menu and running all over town for hard-to-find ingredients. Using my easy recipes and supermarket convenience foods, you can create fabulous dishes in no time—and serve them with style.

Everyday food and decor means anything but ordinary. Faux olive branches and pastas pair with Antipasti and Cappu-tinis at a Tuscan Tryst. Movie night becomes Asian Infused, with dramatic accents, Wild Teriyaki Wings, and Peachy Floats. Cranberry Can Cakes and Sunny Lemonade mix with a palm-tree setting, just like In Palm Springs. And a raft of cool blues, Peach-Mango Cobbler, and Mango Ginger Martinis makes your guests feel they're relaxing By the Lake.

Life is a collection of days, and every one is special, so spend them well with family and friends.

Mediterranean Blue

Remember Tevye, the life-loving character in *Fiddler on the Roof*? That same zest for living inspires this Mediterranean party. Green artichokes take center stage in tall glass vases that sparkle in the candles' glow. Hot, crusty bread plays off kalamata olives in an earthy palette that takes its cue from favorite Greek foods. The table is a tribute to a sunny day. Sky blue hydrangeas and candles capture the colors of the Mediterranean sky, while the table runner, plates, and napkins add billows of cloud white. An awning-striped tablecloth and matching place cards tie blue and white together, setting the stage for accents of garden green. Simple and joyful, this all-occasion party celebrates the many good things in life—good food, good friends, and good times shared in abundance.

Favors: Wrapped in sheer white ribbon and nested in a soup bowl, two light blue taper candles become a take-home memento. A sprig of rosemary, the herb of remembrance, is tucked in the bow to symbolize friendship. **Place Cards:** These echo the tablecloth's summery stripes. Use 3-M™ Spray Mount™ to cover store-bought cards with blue and white striped fabric. Center a white self-adhesive label to the front and pen guests' names in blue ink that matches the blue in the tablecloth.

Santor-tini

- Ice cubes
- 1 shot vanilla vodka, *Absolut*®
- ½ shot pear brandy, *Poire Williams*®
- 1 shot pear nectar, *Del Monte*®
- Champagne, *Korbel*®

1. Fill a martini shaker with ice. Add vodka, brandy, and pear nectar. Shake and strain into martini glass. Top with champagne and serve. Makes 1 drink.

Greek Garden Olives

- 1 cup olive oil, *Bertolli*®
- 4 garlic gloves, whole, rind removed, smashed
- 1 lemon, rind removed and sliced
- 1 cup green olives with pits
- 1 cup kalamata olives with pits
- 2 sprigs fresh oregano
- Ground black pepper

1. Heat oil over low heat. And smashed garlic cloves and slices of lemon rind. Strain olives. Pat dry. Pick off oregano leaves: add to the oil. Add strained olives to oil. Grind fresh pepper over olives. Heat olives through. Makes 2 cups.

Centerpiece: Fresh artichokes, a mainstay in Greek cooking, make a verdant centerpiece showcased in glass cylinder vases, grouped in three sizes for an eye-catching effect.

Accent Pieces: Willowy glass candlesticks and square glass bowls of hydrangeas flank the artichoke vases in sparkling symmetry. Bread dipping bowls filled with oil match the indigo candles.

Food and Drink: Pale, sophisticated Santor-tinis lend the juicy sweetness of pears with dry Champagne. Served in long-stemmed glasses, they counterbalance robust, colorful Greek Garden Olives and crusty bread.

Music: A compilation CD, like *A Mediterranean Odyssey: Athens to Andalusia*, or the sound track from *Fiddler on the Roof* or *My Big Fat Greek Wedding*.

By the Lake

Recreate the simplicity of summers by the shore with a lake lover's palette of soft blues, whites, and splashes of lime green. Birthdays, brunches, or summer Sunday lunches are all good times for a relaxing afternoon getaway. Host the party indoors, and you'll avoid the heat and bugs that come with outdoor picnics. The table is set with casual white plates that bring the blues and greens of the tablecloth to the forefront. Matching no-fuss napkins are simply spread across the plates to create a continuous flow of pattern and color across the tabletop. For dessert, try an old-fashioned peach cobbler like Grandma used to make, updated with a tropical twist of mango. Serve the cobbler in individual dessert dishes set inside miniature enameled colanders. The unexpected serving dishes will delight your guests and add color to the table. To complete your lakeside inside party, just add water—spring water is always a wholesome choice—or refresh your guests with mango martinis enlivened with a kick of ginger.

Centerpiece: A trio of candle lanterns brings the party colors together to cast soft lighting over the table. Blue and white candles add a watercolor effect. **Place Cards:** Mini green and blue colanders become dessert bowls and place cards in one, centered on each plate. Blue hangtags with white name labels match the linens. A shoelace ties the card to the colander. **Accent Pieces:** A timeworn milk carrier puts napkins on display while adding another hint of yesteryear. A lime green metal bucket hosts iced bottles of water.

Peach-Mango Cobbler

1 package (16-ounce) frozen mango chunks, thawed, *Dole®*
1 package (16-ounce) frozen peach slices, thawed, *Dole®*
1 large jalapeño pepper, seeded and diced
¼ cup sugar
2 tablespoons cornstarch, *Argo®*
1 teaspoon cinnamon, *McCormick®*
½ cup butter, divided
1 package sweet corn cake mix, *El Torito®*
Vanilla ice cream (optional), *Häagen Dazs®*

1. In a bowl, combine fruit, jalapeño, sugar, cornstarch, and cinnamon. Stir to coat and let sit for 1 hour.

2. Set up grill for direct cooking over medium heat.

3. In a bowl, blend together ¼ cup of butter and the sweet corn cake mix with a fork until crumbly. Set aside.

4. Place remaining ¼ cup butter in a 10-inch cast-iron skillet (or other ovenproof skillet) and set on hot grill. When butter has melted, add fruit mixture. Stir to combine. Sprinkle corn cake mixture to cover fruit. Cover grill and cook 20 minutes or until mixture is bubbling and caramelized around the edges of the pan.

5. Remove from grill. Serve warm and, if desired, top with a scoop of ice cream. Makes 8 servings.

Indoor Directions: Prepare as above except preheat oven to 350 degrees F. Bake, covered, in preheated oven 20 to 25 minutes or until mixture is bubbling and caramelized around the edges of the pan.

Mango Ginger Martini

Ice cubes
2 shots mango rum, *Cruzan®*
2 shots mango nectar, *Kern's®*
1 teaspoon grated fresh ginger
Champagne, chilled, *Korbel®*

1. Fill a martini shaker with ice cubes. Add rum, mango nectar, and ginger. Shake vigorously. Strain into a martini glass. Top with Champagne. Makes 1 drink.

Food and Drink: It's smooth sailing with an easy-bake Peach-Mango Cobbler cleverly encased in colored colanders. The addition of aromatic ginger takes Mango Ginger Martinis to near nirvana.

Music: Lighthearted jazz is just what the DJ ordered. Try *Jazz Moods: Sounds of Summer* or *Summer Solstice: A Windham Hill Collection*.

In Palm Springs

Soaking up the sun. Lounging by the pool. Cocktails on the terrace. No deadlines, no worries—just friends and fun. In Palm Springs party treats your guests to a little rest and relaxation and some tropical temptations too. To summon that carefree California ambience, dress the table in soothing shades of green and white and lighten up lamps with woven shades. A green tablecloth overlaid with a palm tree runner makes a natural backdrop for palm tree dinnerware, fanned napkins, and wood-handled utensils. These desert accents turn birthdays, Memorial Day, or any spring or summer outing into a mini vacation. In Palm Springs is all about kicking back, so make hostessing a breeze with cooked-in-the can cranberry cakes that double as a centerpiece. Chill out with tall glasses of Sunny Lemonade, spiked with Jack Daniel's®, add some music, and life's little stresses will feel a million miles away.

Dessert Centerpiece: Palm tree pitchers supporting a matching tray become an eye-catching pedestal server for mini cranberry cakes. Serving the cakes in the cans they're baked in makes it stylishly simple. **Place Card:** A palm frond tucked in a ceramic bowl doubles as a party favor and place card. Write each guest's name on a card that has been rubber stamped with a fern and "plant" it in raw sugar "sand." **Favors:** A small rattan recipe box filled with party recipes, tea bags, or even candy makes another souvenir.

Cranberry Can Cakes

- **2 cans (16 ounces each) whole cranberries, *Ocean Spray®***
- **Canola oil cooking spray, *Mazola® Pure®***
- **2 boxes (17.5 ounces each) blueberry muffin mix, *Krusteaz®***
- **2½ cups shredded coconut, toasted, *Baker's®***
- **2 cups white cranberry juice, *Ocean Spray®***
- **2 teaspoons vanilla extract, *McCormick®***
- **2 teaspoons ground cinnamon, *McCormick®***

1. Preheat oven to 400 degrees F. Place cranberries in a strainer; rinse under cold running water. Place in a small bowl. Spray the insides of five 16-ounce cans with cooking spray; set aside.

2. In a large bowl, using a wooden spoon, stir together drained cranberries, muffin mix, coconut, cranberry juice, vanilla, and cinnamon. Divide mixture among the prepared cans; place cans on a baking sheet.

3. Using oven mitts, place baking sheet in preheated oven. Bake for 30 to 35 minutes or until a toothpick inserted in center of a cake comes out clean. Using oven mitts, remove from oven. Place cans on a wire rack. Cool completely.

4. With a table knife, loosen edges of cakes by running knife between cakes and edges of cans. Remove cakes by inverting cans. Wrap cakes in plastic wrap. To serve, place cakes back in cans. Makes 5 cakes.

Mini Cake Containers: Gather empty cans and clean them thoroughly. Bake cakes and let cool. Wrap with decorative fabric and secure it in the back with hook-and-loop tape. Tie raffia ribbon or twine around the top and bottom, and you've got a tasty tropical treat.

Sunny Lemonade

- **1 shot whiskey, *Jack Daniel's®***
- **2 tablespoons lemonade frozen concentrate, *Minute Maid®***
- **5 ice cubes**
- **1 cup lemon-lime soda, *Sprite®***
- **Maraschino cherry, for garnish**

1. Pour whiskey and lemonade concentrate into a highball glass. Stir. Add ice cubes and fill glass with soda.

2. Garnish with a maraschino cherry. Makes 1 drink.

Music: Get those good vibrations going with the Beach Boys' *Endless Summer* CD or pack a vacation vibe with a Caribbean or salsa mix. *Frank Sinatra Sings Cole Porter* is another In Palm Springs choice.

Tuscan Tryst

My love of Italy began in childhood, when I was captivated by a picture I saw in a book. The green hills, scarlet grapes, and fiery Tuscan sun contrasted so vividly with my home in the misty Pacific Northwest. I realized that there was a whole world out there, just waiting to be experienced and savored. As an adult, I got my first taste of Tuscany and felt a deep appreciation for the region's artisanship and hospitality. An Italian tablescape is always built around food—golden breads and pastas, rich red and green antipasti, and creamy Cappu-tinis. I softened the traditional red, green, and white of the Italian flag to muted shades of mint and red, accented with pale golds and ivories, to create an easygoing ambience. A paisley cloth makes a genteel backdrop for rustic green pottery, and matching ties trimmed with elaborate tassels wrap the red napkins. Simple foods double as the decor, keeping the focus on the things I've learned Italians value most—food and family, a fitting tribute to Italy, the land of the grape.

Place Setting: The fabric for the tablecloth and napkin ties nearly matches the soft green of the dishware, creating a quiet, relaxed effect. Paprika-color napkins and flatware pick up the touch of red in the fabric. Unusual serving dishes like the leaf-shape bowl make surprising soup bowls.

Place Card Party Favors: Fruit-of-the-vine place cards are a take-home toast to Italy's many vineyards. Purchase sheets of colored paper that coordinates with your tablecloth and narrow ribbon that matches your napkins. To make each favor, cut the paper into a rectangle and punch a hole in one end. Thread a length of ribbon through the hole, wrap it around the cork of a mini wine bottle, and secure with a knot. Using matching ribbon, tie the cork and place card around the neck of the wine bottle. Write the guest's name on the paper to complete the place card.

Fashion: Cozy and understated are the keywords. A soft sweater and casual pants in the party's muted shades fit the mood.

Food and Drink: Colorful Antipasti picks up the red, green, and white palette. Coffee-rich Cappu-tinis blend right in, offering guests an Italian interpretation of the classic martini.

Centerpiece: An olive jar vase filled with olive branches, glass canisters of uncooked pasta, and ivory tapers in corkscrew candlesticks blend Italy's rich artisan heritage with a love of food and family.

Accent Pieces: Leaf-shape plates accentuate the importance of fresh ingredients in Italian cooking. Shaped pastas like linguine, fusilli (corkscrew pasta) and farfalle (bow tie pasta) provide interesting texture in lidded jars. Curvy shapes give simple pottery pieces and plain glass stemware an air of elegance.

Music: It wouldn't be authentically Italian without someone singing "That's Amore!" *Viva Italia—Festive Italian Classics* sets an upbeat tone, or play *Mandolins from Italy* for a softer, more romantic occasion.

Cappu-tini

- Ice cubes
- 2 shots Frappuccino® coffee drink, ***Starbucks®***
- 1 shot vodka, ***Absolut®***

1. Fill a martini shaker with ice cubes. Add coffee drink and vodka. Shake vigorously. Strain into a martini glass. Makes 1 drink.

Antipasti

- 1 bag (5-ounce) mixed torn salad greens, ***Fresh Express®***
- 1 pound assorted deli meats (such as salami, mortadella ham, cappocola)
- 1 container (8-ounce) fresh mozzarella cheese, ***Fiorella Fresh®***
- 4 ounces provolone cheese, sliced
- 1 jar (16-ounce) mixed olives, ***Giuliano Olive Antipasto®***
- 2 tomatoes, quartered
- 1 cup pepperoncini
- 1 can (15-ounce) garbanzo beans, rinsed and drained, ***Progresso®***
- 1 cup (½ bottle) balsamic vinaigrette, ***Newman's Own®***
- Packaged breadsticks

1. Place greens on a large platter. Arrange deli meats, cheeses, olives, tomatoes, pepperoncini, and garbanzo beans on top. Drizzle with vinaigrette. Serve with breadsticks. Makes 4 servings.

Cheese & Wine Fête

While a wine tasting is often thought of as a more formal affair, this lighthearted get-together puts a casual spin on it. Edibles and drinkables are the marquee attraction, so start with a tray of assorted cheeses and palate-cleansing fruits, then pour on the fun with a selection of wines. Guests enjoy learning about new wines, so display cards with a wine's name, region, and flavor (dry, sweet, etc.) in front of the bottle. Encourage guests to experiment with different flavors by recommending cheeses that enhance each wine's bouquet. When it comes to decor, roosters rule. A popular collectible in the '30s and '40s, roosters have become trendy again as a country French favorite. Look for paper roosters and tableware at party stores or scout antiques stores for vintage ceramic roosters. A black and cream check fabric grounds a wine-centric color scheme of reds, golds, and browns to create a nostalgic setting for birthdays and "just for fun" evenings with friends. Present the place setting with panache by layering clear glass plates over rooster motif chargers and resting the charger on a napkin-draped woven tray.

Decorative Decor: Roosters fit right in with the rustic decor. If you have trouble finding rooster accessories in your local stores, check garage sales and thrift shops or change the motif to a collectible you already own. Birdhouses, birds, or apples all complement a country motif. Rooster tea light lamps cast ambient light through cutout shades, and French wire baskets can hold fruit, cheese, and crackers.

Hot Spiced Sangria

2 bottles (750 ml each) Rioja (Spanish red wine)
2 bottles (750 ml each) white wine
1 cup brandy, *Christian Brothers®*
1 orange, sliced
2 cups frozen cherries, *Dole®*
2 cups frozen peaches, *Dole®*
2 cinnamon sticks, *McCormick®*
1 cup simple syrup*
Cinnamon sticks, for garnish, *McCormick®*

1. Combine all ingredients, except cinnamon stick garnish, in 4½- to 5-quart slow cooker.

2. Put setting on HIGH setting for 1 hour. Reduce to warm to hold temperature. Ladle into glasses from slow cooker. Be sure to include some fruit in the glasses. Garnish each glass with a cinnamon stick. Makes 12 drinks.
***Note:** To make a simple syrup, combine 1 cup sugar with 1 cup water in a saucepan. Bring to a boil; reduce to a simmer. Stirring occasionally, simmer for 5 minutes or until sugar is dissolved.

Centerpiece: The scent of flowers can interfere with a wine's bouquet, so it's better to opt for a fruit centerpiece. A rustic basket of red apples and pears keeps the focus on the aromatic wines and cheeses.

Accent Pieces: Rooster tea light lamps cast twinkling light through cutout shades. Wooden cutting boards and wooden or woven baskets can hold fruit, cheese, and crackers. Feathered roosters add authentic country French touches.

Mini Box Place Card Favors: Buy corrugated cardboard mini boxes at a craft store. (If the boxes come with lids, save those for another project.) To add texture, use double-stick tape to wrap the box with a wide copper-tone ribbon. Pen each guest's name on a self-adhesive label and stick one label to the front of each box. Fill boxes with wood shavings, nest a plastic or ceramic rooster inside, and you've got a fab favor.

Music: Classical background music or a soft jazz works best. Select instrumentals from the same region as your wines. Lower the volume to facilitate lively discussions about each wine's merits.

Apple Cinnamon Bread Pudding

Canola oil cooking spray, *Mazola® Pure®*
3 beaten eggs
2 cups milk, cream, or a combination
1½ teaspoons rum extract, *McCormick®*
½ teaspoon salt
¼ cup brown sugar
6 cups raisin bread, cubed (about 15 slices)
1 can (20.5-ounce) apple pie filling, *Comstock® More Fruit*
½ cup raisins
2 packets cinnamon roll instant oatmeal, *Quaker® Oats*

1. Preheat oven to 350 degrees F. Spray a 2-quart baking dish with spray; set aside.

2. In a bowl, whisk together eggs, milk, rum extract, salt, and brown sugar. Stir in raisin bread, pie filling, raisins, and oatmeal packets until bread cubes are moist.

3. Pour the mixture into prepared baking dish. Bake in preheated oven for 30 to 40 minutes or until pudding has risen and browned and a knife inserted into the center comes out clean. Makes 8 servings.

Food and Drink: Seedless grapes and sliced pears and apples complement a collection of mild and strong cheeses, like nutty Parmigiano Reggiano, creamy Brie, and pungent Maytag blue. Apple Cinnamon Bread Pudding and Hot Spiced Sangria end the evening on a sweet, smooth note.

Asian Infused

Any night is a good night when you take-out in. You don't need to wait for a special occasion—just keep the accent on fun with a bold red and black color scheme and a fusion of Asian food and accessories. The secret is to order the main dishes from your favorite Chinese restaurant. Check a day or so ahead to see how much time to allow, then call in your order and let the restaurant do the work. With takeout headlining the menu, you're free to focus on a scene-stealing table. Dish up the drama with square red and black plates set atop bamboo place mats over a vivid red tablecloth. A white table runner stamped with Chinese characters, black bamboo steamers, and mini kimonos cloaking red napkins add Asian appeal. Crudités make quick appetizers, especially when you buy the veggies precut and cleaned. To give your guests a wok on the wild side, zap up some Wild Teriyaki Wings with a tale of two sauces—veggie or peanut. Purchased fortune cookies and dreamy Peachy Floats make a fuss-free finale.

Napkin/Chopstick Holders: Look for miniature Asian-style jackets in craft or hobby stores or search online for a wide variety of low-cost options. To make, tightly fold or roll the napkin, then slip the chopsticks and napkin upward through the hem of the jacket and out the neckline.

Peachy Floats

1 can (15-ounce) canned sliced peaches, *Del Monte*®
1 shot peach schnapps (optional), *DeKuyper*®
1 pint peaches and cream ice cream, *Häagen-Dazs*®
Lemon-lime soda, *Sprite*®

1. Place 3 peach slices into a large glass. If desired, add peach schnapps. Top with 2 scoops of ice cream. Slowly fill glass with lemon-lime soda. Serve with straw. Makes 4 drinks.

Centerpiece: Food is the star of this table. A bamboo bench puts colorful appetizers and votive candleholders filled with dipping sauces within ready reach. Hook a tasseled Chinese lantern on your light fixture to draw attention to the food.

Accent Pieces: Red platters on upside-down vases moonlight as pedestal servers, while decorative take-out containers make festive decor. (Or fill them with fortune cookies and send them home as favors.) Add a touch of the Orient with a towering wicker birdcage and ornate lacquered chopsticks.

Music: Get in a movie mood with the *Mikado* cast recording or the *Memoirs of a Geisha* soundtrack. Or preview the upcoming attraction by playing the soundtrack from the film you're screening.

Nacho Potatoes

- **1 can (2¼-ounce) sliced black olives, *Early California®***
- **½ bag (22-ounce) waffle fries, *Ore-Ida®***
- **1 can (16-ounce) refried black bean beans, *Rosarita®***
- **1 cup Mexican cheese blend, *Kraft®***
- **½ cup mild chunky salsa, *Pace®***
- **½ cup dairy sour cream, *Knudsen®***

1. Preheat oven to 400 degrees F. Line a baking sheet with aluminum foil; set aside. Using a strainer set over a small bowl, drain olives; set aside. Discard liquid.

2. Arrange potatoes in a single layer on prepared baking sheet. Using oven mitts, place baking sheet in preheated oven. Bake for 18 to 20 minutes.

3. While fries are baking, spoon black beans into a microwave-safe bowl. Cover bowl loosely with plastic wrap. Place in microwave. Cook on 100 percent power (HIGH) for 4 to 6 minutes. Using oven mitts, remove from microwave. Cool about 5 minutes. Carefully remove plastic wrap.

4. To assemble, evenly space potatoes on a microwave-safe plate. Top each with 1 tablespoon beans and a sprinkle of cheese. Place in microwave. Cook, uncovered, on 100 percent power (HIGH) for 1 minute or until cheese is melted.

5. Top each stack with 1 teaspoon salsa, 1 teaspoon sour cream, and an olive slice. Makes 4 servings.

Wild Teriyaki Wings

3 pounds chicken drumettes, *Foster Farms®*
1 tablespoon salt
1 teaspoon ground black pepper
1 bottle (10-ounce) teriyaki marinade, *Kikkoman®*
1 can (8-ounce) crushed pineapple, *Dole®*
2 tablespoons sesame seeds (optional), *McCormick®*
1 recipe Veggie Dipping Sauce (see recipe below)
1 recipe Peanut Dipping Sauce (see recipe below)

1. Preheat oven to 400 degrees F. Line baking sheet with aluminum foil; set aside.

2. Season chicken drumettes with salt and pepper.

3. Place chicken in large zip-top plastic bag. Pour teriyaki marinade and undrained crushed pineapple into the bag. Squeeze out excess air from bag and seal. Massage ingredients in bag. Place bag in refrigerator; chill for 1 hour to marinate.

4. Remove drumettes from bag; discard marinade. Arrange drumettes evenly on baking sheet.

5. Place baking sheet in preheated oven. Bake for 40 minutes. Remove from oven. Place drumettes on a serving plate. If desired, sprinkle with sesame seeds. Serve with sauces. Makes 18 servings.

Timesaving Tips: Set the table with paper plates, napkins, and plastic utensils for a speedy cleanup. Bake the Wild Teriyaki Wings the day before and refrigerate. Heat just before serving. **For Veggie Dipping Sauce, *above middle:*** In a small bowl, using a spoon, combine 1 container (8-ounce) light garden vegetable cream cheese, *Philadelphia®* and 1 cup dairy sour cream, *Knudsen®*. Cover with plastic wrap. Chill in the refrigerator. **For Peanut Dipping Sauce, *above middle:*** In a small bowl, using a spoon, combine 1 cup creamy peanut butter, *Laura Scudder's®*, 1 cup plain yogurt, *Dannon®*, and 2 tablespoons frozen limeade concentrate, thawed, *Minute Maid®*. Cover with plastic wrap. Chill in the refrigerator until ready to serve. Each recipe makes 2 cups. Fresh veggies, *above left*, add color. Fortune cookies, *above right*, can ignite interesting conversations among your guests.

Geranium Garden

Geraniums are one of my favorite flowers. They're easy to find, easy to grow, and come in a lot of lively colors—like this vibrant red, sure to put guests in a party mood. Paired with fresh whites and greens, the look is pure vintage charm, a fragrant way to celebrate the arrival of spring—or anything else. Add just the right note of nostalgia to everyday gatherings or create a garden oasis for special celebrations like wedding showers, family reunions, or a best friend's birthday. Give your tablescape that in-the-garden feeling with greenhouse florals, picnic plaids, and old-timey tea towels. Cheerful and homey is the tone, from the red and white place settings to masses of red geraniums that fill the room with color and fragrance. (Faux flowers will work too.) Red whets the appetite, as so many restaurants know, so dish up plenty of comfort food, like an old-fashioned Cherry Crumble, updated with cherry brandy and gingersnaps. Pair with Café Roma Martinis, flavored with a shot of sambuca to make a cool coffee alternative.

Window Treatments: The colorful flower-bedecked print in the tablecloth is the same fabric used in the pleated window treatments, premade and store-bought for ease, or if you like to sew, have a go at making them.

Favors: A recipe box makes a take-home garden covered with floral fabric and topped with a packet of tomato seeds tied to a sprig of geraniums. Trim with red ribbon to delight gardeners of all ages.

Centerpiece: Twin tins filled with red geraniums mirror the napkin rings to add subtle shine centertable. The buffet table repeats the motif with potted geraniums flanking a silver bucket holding bottles of white wine.

Place Settings: A flower-sprigged tablecloth makes a garden-fresh backdrop for red and white plates set picnic-style on galvanized plant pot saucers. White napkins spring to life tied with geraniums and seed packets.

Place Cards: Tin cups filled with mini gardening tools will rake in the compliments. Use a red pen to write each guest's name on a red-bordered self-adhesive label.

Accent Pieces: A lipstick red colander plays host to party favors—cherry tomato seed packets hole-punched to hold a ribbon-tied geranium. A galvanized potting bench makes a self-serve bar. Even the simple pleated window treatment matches the tablecloth, pulling the whole room together.

Music: *Broadway: America's Music 1935-2005* takes you through almost a century of sentimental favorites.

Cherry Crumble

Slow-Cooked Cherries
1 bag (16-ounce) frozen cherries, *C&W*®
1 cup sugar
¾ cup water
½ cup dried cherries, *Mariani*®
¼ cup cherry brandy, *Hiram Walker*®
2 tablespoons quick-cooking tapioca, *Minute*®
Crumble Topping
¾ cup low-fat granola, *Quaker*® *100% Natural*
½ cup baking mix, *Bisquick*®
10 gingersnaps, crushed, *Nabisco*®
2 tablespoons butter, melted
Vanilla ice cream, (optional), *Häagen Dazs*®

1. For the Slow-Cooked Cherries, in a 4-quart slow cooker, stir together frozen cherries, sugar, water, dried cherries, brandy, and tapioca. Cover and cook on HIGH heat setting for 2 to 4 hours.

2. For the Crumble Topping, 30 minutes before fruit is ready, preheat oven to 350 degrees F. Line a baking sheet with aluminum foil; set aside.

3. In a medium bowl, stir together granola, baking mix, gingersnaps, and melted butter. Spread evenly on prepared baking sheet. Bake in preheated oven for 12 to 18 minutes or until crisp and golden.

4. To serve, spoon Slow-Cooked Cherries into dessert dishes. Sprinkle with Crumble Topping. If desired, top each serving with a scoop of ice cream. Makes 8 servings.

Café Roma Martini

1 shot sambuca
1 shot coffee liqueur, *Kahlúa*®
1 shot half-and-half
Ice cubes
Coffee beans, for garnish

1. Add all ingredients, except garnish, to a cocktail shaker filled with ice. Shake well and strain into martini glass. Garnish with 3 coffee beans. Makes 1 drink.

Daisy Delight

Roses may be beautiful, orchids elegant, but delightful daisies win hands-down for homey charm. A daisy-theme party brings a sweet, innocent attitude to everyday entertaining—just the mood for an all-girl gathering, whether it's a birthday brunch, afternoon tea, baby shower, or simply a celebration of spring. The palette is fresh and sunny and not the least bit fussy—like the unassuming daisy itself—with crisp whites and yellows interspersed with a garden of greens that range from glossy to a soft Key lime. The foundation is a family of daisy dinnerware and accessories, accented with a scattering of faux or fresh daisies that bring the pattern to life. Add to that a double-layer table dressing of a soft lime-and-white-striped topper over a lime green tablecloth and the stage is set. Best of all, the menu is deliciously uncomplicated. What else would you expect from the simple daisy? Toast the guest of honor (or just each other) with all-ages-appropriate Tropical Granita Cocktails and finish with a cool Lemon Sorbet, served in dainty green glass bowls and garnished with fresh mint. Even when the party's over, every guest's heart will be as light as a child's. Daisies just seem to have that effect on us—all year-round.

Window Treatment: Sunlight streaming in the window looks even prettier framed in flowers. Buy sheer daisy trim by the yard at your local fabric store. Create a fun streamer effect by cutting varying lengths of it and either thumbtacking or stapling them to a piece of green fabric or an inexpensive valance or window shade. You can use the same material to match the window to the tablecloth or mix it up a bit with a coordinating pattern.

Centerpiece: The centerpiece does double duty as both a drink server and decoration. A cake stand placed on top of a large, upside-down serving bowl showcases beverages. Make each sip special with a fresh wedge of pineapple on the edge of the glass and faux daisies hot-glued to yellow and green ribbons tied around the stem.

Place Settings: Stacking different size plates creates eye-pleasing rings of flowers. Top them off with a pretty white napkin gathered with a daisy ponytail holder. Or make your own napkin ring by hot-gluing a faux daisy to a ribbon tied around the napkin. The soft green Lucite®-handled flatware ties in beautifully to the green colors.

Favors: I love to send guests home with a personal party favor—such as a box filled with treats. This one was made by painting an unfinished craft store recipe box in party colors. Buy one box for each guest, then paint them—the base a delicious Key lime green, the top a meringue white—then fill them with take-home treats such as candy or cookies. Tie the boxes up vertically and horizontally with sheer daisy-dotted ribbon so they look like presents. Working vertically, hot glue the ribbon across the bottom and up the sides, tucking the ends inside the box and affixing them inside with hot glue. Do the same horizontally. On the lid, hot glue ribbon vertically and horizontally, tucking all ends under the lid and hot-gluing them there. Tie a beautiful bow and affix it on the top middle of the lid with hot glue. Embellish the front of the box with a faux daisy hot-glued to the ribbon.

Place Cards: Invite guests with charming place cards. Place two squares of yellow and green paper together with the yellow paper on top and the green paper, slightly larger, beneath. Write the guest's name on the yellow square with a green pen. Punch a hole in the upper left corner of both squares, poke the stem of a faux daisy through the holes, tuck the flower into a coffee cup, and put at place settings.

Accent Pieces: Spread cheer by the pitcher, pot, or basket. Fill white ceramic pitchers with lush lemon branches, greenery, and dainty white blossoms. Faux daisies in yellow pots are slipped into French wire cachepots that bring the garden freshness indoors.

Tropical Granita Cocktails

- **1 can (20-ounce) crushed pineapple (juice pack), *Dole®***
- **1 can (11.5-ounce) papaya nectar, *Kerns®***
- **2 tablespoons frozen limeade concentrate, *Minute Maid®***
- **1 teaspoon coconut extract, *McCormick®***
- **Fresh pineapple wedges (optional)**

1. In a bowl, combine undrained crushed pineapple, papaya nectar, limeade concentrate, and coconut extract. Spoon into a 13×9-inch baking dish. Freeze for at least 6 hours or overnight.

2. To serve, use a fork to scrape mixture into an icy consistency. Spoon into glasses. If desired, garnish with fresh pineapple wedges. Makes 4 drinks.

Lemon Sorbet

- **1 tablespoon sugar-free, low-calorie lemon gelatin dessert mix, *Jell-O®***
- **1 cup boiling water**
- **1 cup cold water**
- **1 cup frozen lemonade concentrate, thawed, *Minute Maid®***
- **Fresh mint sprigs, for garnish (optional)**

1. In a mixing bowl, stir gelatin into boiling water until completely dissolved (about 2 minutes) When gelatin is completely dissolved, stir in cold water and lemonade concentrate until blended. Cover with plastic wrap and cool in refrigerator for 30 minutes.

2. Pour lemon mixture into 1-quart ice cream maker and freeze according to manufacturer's instructions. When sorbet is frozen, transfer to an airtight container and freeze at least 2 hours. If desired, garnish each serving with a mint sprig. Makes 8 servings.

Special Days

It's known as "hospitality"—the art of graciously opening our homes and sharing the foods of our table, with family, friends, and, sometimes, strangers. The food we share reflects who we are. As a child, I squeezed lemonade and baked berry cobbler for my younger brothers and sisters. In college, Colleen and I grilled bratwurst in beer for tailgates. As adults, we all enjoy fine wines and cheeses for an evening soirée. Fit the food to the occasion for a day that will always be special.

Semi-Homemade® helps you make any occasion one to remember, whether it's a casual Labor Day Cookout or a Romantic Day Picnic with a basket ã deux. What you'll not remember is days of prep time, because every single recipe can be made, and served, in minutes.

Special days deserve extra sparkle. This chapter is filled with beautiful food and simple touches that give your table personality without emptying your wallet. Borrow a blue theme for an Anniversary Affair, made effortlessly elegant with Peach-Pepper Veal Chops and Lemony Haricots Verts. Whether it's Cinco de Mayo—or Quattro de Abril—stained-glass colors turn Petite Lime Cheesecakes and Cosmoritas into a full-blown fiesta. Strawberries and freesia, Champagne Parfaits, and Passion Fruit Martinis convey Mother's Day love to a special mom, while fast cars and even faster food—on the grill—pay a Father's Day tribute to dear old dad. Food. Friends. Family. And a fabulous beverage. That's all it takes to make any day special.

Aunt Sandy and Stephanie stroll along the beach, while Bryce builds castles in the sand.

Sara

An Anniversary Affair

White lace and promises—that's how it all started and is revisited again in a romantic palette that hints at that glorious wedding day years ago. Combine soft whites with true blues and you'll have the perfect color scheme to toast everlasting love. Or reinterpret the setting to celebrate all kinds of life-enhancing relationships, from Mother's Day and birthdays to luncheons and afternoon tea. The chandeliers, etched glasses, and clear trumpet vases sparkle like white diamonds, yet the splendor is anchored by the charm of the floral print tablecloth and mismatched china. Old, new, borrowed, and blue mix in a panoply of patterns that harmonize beautifully, thanks to their familiar colors and small-scale patterns. For the menu, try something a bit unexpected. Veal chops, a rare and wonderful treat in restaurants, bring elegance home, surprising and exceeding expectations when brushed with a luscious peach-pepper glaze. Paired with Lemony Haricots Verts, they bring fresh color to a lovely table.

Place Settings: A sleek white charger is topped with two patterns of classic blue-and-white plates. The scalloped edge of the fluted middle plate echoes the crochet-edge napkin, which is loosely fanned and tied with a knotted blue organza ribbon. Embossed glasses add another layer of elegance and texture.

Lee

Centerpiece: The graceful trumpet vases exude refinement and the white silk lilies that bring on the romance. Whatever flowers you choose, be sure they're tall and generously proportioned, as wispier stems will be overpowered by the vase.

Place Cards: The ceramic place cards can be used again and again. Simply pen guests' names in blue ink, then after the party, wipe them clean and store until next time.

Accent Pieces: The blue border on the tiered serving pedestal ties the eclecticism of the dinnerware together. The tiers are topped with ready-made foods—coconut layer cake on the bottom, white chocolate-covered sandwich cookies and white meringue kisses in the center, and party favors on top. Scour secondhand stores for candlesticks in a variety of shapes and sizes—I snatched up an armload of these for only a dollar apiece.

Favors: The tiered server is topped with petite packages of Jordan almonds wrapped in lace-edged handkerchiefs and tied with a sheer ribbon to mirror the dinner napkins. These dainty favors are both decoration and takeaway.

Music: Something sweet and slightly nostalgic fits the mood. Ken Griffin's *Anniversary Song/Skating Time* and Norah Jones' *Come Away with Me* create a happy atmosphere.

Fashion: My classic blue-and-white outfit echoes the color scheme. The scoop-neck top taps into the romance of it all while crushed cords say easy and relaxed.

Peach-Pepper Veal Chops

Veal Chops
1 can (11.5-ounce) peach nectar, *Kern's*®
1 packet (12-ounce) black peppercorn marinade mix, *Durkee*® *Grill Creations*®
4½ pounds veal loin chops
Glaze
½ cup peach jam, *Smucker's*®
¼ cup bourbon, *Jim Beam*®
1 tablespoon cracked black peppercorns

1. For the chops, in a large zip-top plastic bag, combine peach nectar, marinade mix, and veal chops. Squeeze out air and seal bag. Massage bag to ensure chops are coated. Refrigerate 3 to 6 hours to marinate.

2. For the glaze, in a small saucepan over medium heat, combine jam, bourbon, and cracked peppercorns. Bring to boil, reduce heat and simmer for 10 minutes. Remove from heat; set aside.

3. Set up grill for direct cooking over medium-high heat. Oil grate when ready to start cooking.

4. Remove chops from marinade and bring to room temperature (about 20 minutes). Discard marinade.

5. Grill chops on hot oiled grill for 4 to 5 minutes. Turn and brush with glaze. Cook an additional 4 to 5 minutes. Turn and glaze; cook for 1 minute. Remove from heat and brush once more with glaze. Serve hot. Makes 4 servings.

Lemony Haricots Verts

12 ounces frozen haricots verts or petite green beans, *C&W*®
1 tablespoon butter
2 teaspoons shredded lemon zest
1 teaspoon lemon-pepper seasoning, *Lawry's*®
Salt and ground black pepper

1. In a microwave-safe bowl, combine frozen beans, butter, lemon zest, and lemon pepper. Cover with plastic wrap; microwave on 100 percent power (HIGH) for 4 minutes. Stir; cook for 3 to 4 minutes more. Season with salt and pepper to taste. Makes 4 servings.

Romantic Day Picnic

Recapture the days of courtly love, when brave knights declared their devotion to ladies fair, and everyone indulged in the civilized pleasures of life—good food, fine wine, and words from the heart. To bridge yesterday with today, set a seductive spread on vintage floral tablecloths, arranged picnic style on the grass. Grace your makeshift table with antique plates, urnlike chalices, rusty wire mesh baskets, and silverware that looks generations old. (Who's going to know it came from the thrift store?) If you have old silver, use it. No need to polish a thing—a bit of tarnish here and there ups the rustic romance. The rich neutral palette—a rhapsody of golds, creams, and browns—goes beautifully with the yellowed pages, bronzed metals, and a wicker picnic hamper filled with fruits and cheeses. (Slip a tray inside and you can serve right from it.) The crimson-glazed game hens, glistening grapes, and a plate of strawberries enliven the scene with beats of red—it is, after all, the color of the heart. Round out the menu with flakey Cheese Palmiers pastries, a chocolate bonbon and a bottle of your best champagne—a wonderful way to pour out your love to your own knight in shining armor.

Decorative Details: Scour collectibles shops and thrift stores for old books of poetry to use as decor. Tear out pages of romantic passages, burn the edges, and hot-glue each page to a weathered metal plate to make a distinctive accent. Stack extra books to create a pedestal for food. **Fashion:** Dress casual but classic. My tan slacks mesh well with the scene's timeworn metallics, and the ribbed scoop-neck sweater adds to the romance.

Centerpiece: Displaying textured pale-color flowers in a woven basket is softer than a vase. The trick is to arrange the flowers in a glass bowl first. Cut floral foam to line the bottom, tuck in the flowers, then position the bowl inside the basket. The picnic basket repeats the weave.

Place Settings: Decorative, metal serving vessels, like the plates and goblets here, are generally not food safe. Line them with clear glass containers or plates to serve food—the glass "disappears," letting the soft verdigris patina shine through. Vintage rhinestone belt buckles stand in for napkin rings, accessorizing pale gold napkins like luxurious crown jewels.

Accent Pieces: The French call them billets-doux—sweet little notes passed secretly between lovers. To make your own, rip pages from old books, tie each with a mocha ribbon, and stack the scrolls in a French wire basket. Heighten the old world feel with stacks of books and pillar candles set on chunky distressed pedestals.

Music: Classical music is poetry to the ear. A collection of piano or violin concertos by the great romantics, like Vivaldi's *The Four Seasons* or Itzhak Perlman's *Greatest Hits*, is the ideal accompaniment for such an amorous setting.

Tangerine Glazed Game Hens

3 Cornish game hens, *Tyson*®
Salt
Black pepper
Wood chips, soaked in water
1½ cups tangerine juice, *Odwalla*®
2 tablespoons honey, *SueBee*®
⅓ cup dry white wine
2 tablespoons ginger teriyaki marinade mix, *McCormick*® *Grill Mates*®

1. Set up grill for indirect cooking (no heat source under birds) using medium heat.

2. Cut hens in half with kitchen shears, removing backbones. Rinse with cold water and pat dry. Season both sides of halves with salt and pepper.

3. Put drained wood chips over coals or in smoke box. Place hen halves, bone sides down, on grill over drip pan. Cover grill and cook 1 hour to 1 hour 15 minutes or until thigh temperature registers 180 degrees F.

4. While hens are cooking, prepare glaze by reducing tangerine juice by half in a small pot over medium-high heat. Once juice is reduced, stir in honey, wine, and teriyaki mix. Bring to boil and remove from heat.

5. About 20 minutes before hens are done, brush liberally with glaze every 10 minutes.

6. Remove from grill and let rest 10 minutes before serving, brush with glaze once more. Serve hot. Makes 4 servings.

Indoor method: Preheat oven to 425 degrees F. Prepare glaze as directed. Place seasoned hens in a roasting pan, skin sides up. Pour glaze over hens and roast in preheated oven for 40 to 45 minutes until thigh temperature registers 180 degrees F, basting every 15 minutes.

Cheese Palmiers

6 tablespoons grated Parmesan cheese, divided, *DiGiorno*®
½ box (17.3-ounce) frozen puff pastry (1 sheet), thawed, *Pepperidge Farm*®
1 egg, lightly beaten with 1 tablespoon water
¼ cup shredded Italian cheese blend, *Kraft*®
1 teaspoon paprika, *McCormick*®

1. Sprinkle work surface with 1 tablespoon grated Parmesan cheese.

2. Unfold thawed puff pastry sheet on Parmesan cheese. Lightly brush with egg wash.

3. In a medium bowl, combine 2 tablespoons Parmesan cheese, Italian cheese blend, and paprika. Sprinkle over surface of pastry sheet. Lightly press cheese into pastry.

4. Fold top and bottom edges of pastry to the center. Next, fold in half from left to right. Then, fold in half top to bottom. Place on a plate and refrigerate at least 30 minutes or as long as overnight.

5. Preheat oven to 400 degrees F. Line baking sheet with parchment paper; set aside.

6. Cut ⅛-inch thick slices starting at the short edge. Dip "faces" of palmiers in remaining Parmesan cheese and lay "face up" on prepared baking sheet 2 inches apart.

7. Bake in preheated oven for 20 minutes. Serve warm or at room temperature. Makes 12 servings.

Cinco de Mayo Fiesta

Olé! The mood of this Cinco de Mayo party is so joyous, you'll be tempted to call on its vivid colors and festive flavors again and again throughout the year. And why not? Cinco de Mayo originally celebrated Mexico's victory over the French, so go ahead and parlay this party into a celebration of success—at the office, on the ball field, or come a birthday to celebrate the start of another year. Forgo the shooters, and you'll have a gleeful setting for a kids' taco party or a graduation fiesta for the holder of that new diploma. Whatever the reason, rule numero uno is to use bright, bold colors. That's easily said, and easily done, when you start with the most summery striped piece of cloth you can rustle up at the fabric store. Don't worry about doing any hemming. This is a sewing-free idea—just fit it on and top with a montage of plates in full-fiesta colors. Start the festivities with sparkling Cosmoritas and signal a grande finale with refreshing Petite Lime Cheesecakes that are pretty enough to stand in for a centerpiece. Toss some pillows on benches to bring in even more color—and entice guests to settle in and stay a while.

Accent Pieces: Tequila shooters liven things up, especially when served in waves of sand. Pour colored play sand into wavy stripes in a shallow glass dish and nestle etched-glass shot glasses in the sand. A whitewashed cathedral candle stand makes a Gothic backdrop; its bubble-glass votives in stained-glass hues recall quaint churches in a Mexican town square. **Fashion:** A gauzy white skirt is the epitome of breezy style, while a textured open-weave top adds waves of color.

Alex
Tom

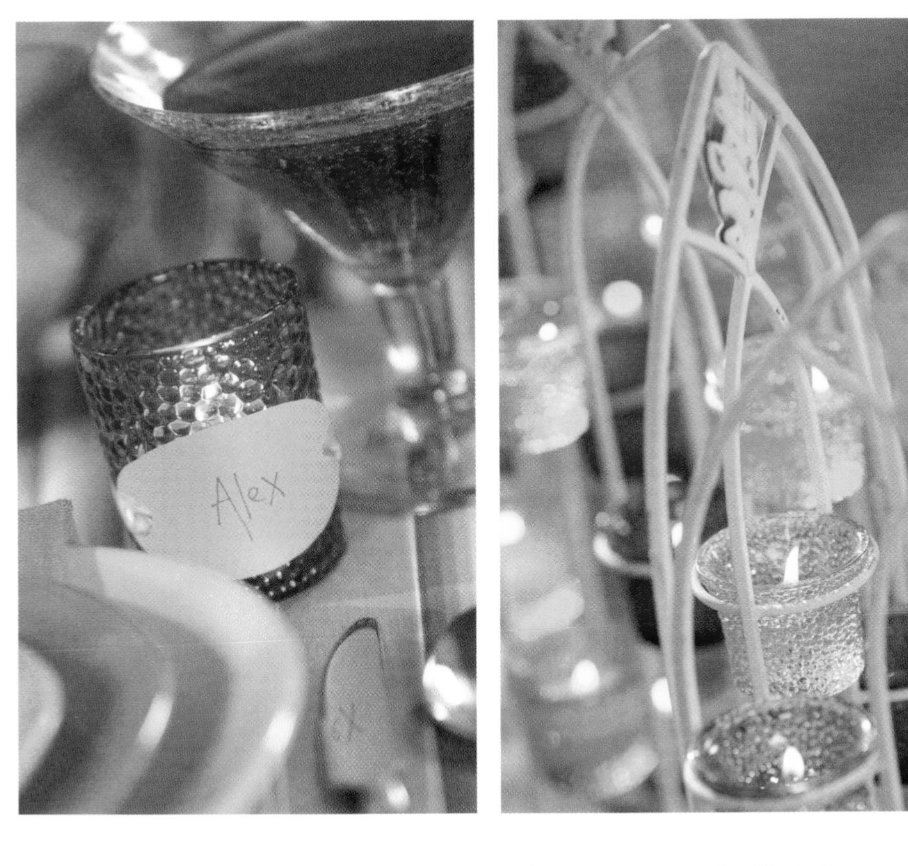

Place Settings: Get the party going with Fiesta® Ware plates stacked in fruity flavors, like tangerine, melon, lemon, and lime, with a plaid kitchen towel tucked in between as a napkin. Set a paper cocktail napkin on the top plate to add another burst of color and top that with a vibrant party favor. Finish with Lucite®-handled flatware in a rainbow of primary shades. (Catch it on sale at party or home stores.)

Centerpiece: A sombrero centerpiece puts dessert on a pedestal. Wrap a cake stand in an extra dishtowel (to match the napkins) and rest a green straw hat on top. Add a colorful plate of mini lime cheesecakes as the crowning touch.

Favors: A flowering cactus goes home with each guest. I found these cute ceramic cubes at a craft store and was delighted to find that a mini flowerpot slipped right inside the hole. Spray paint the terra-cotta pots and plant a cactus inside for a takeaway favor.

Place Cards: Turn extra votive candles into mood-enhancing place cards. Use a cookie cutter to cut colored paper into ovals. Write the guest's name on the front and punch holes on both sides; thread a ribbon through the holes and around the votive, tying in the back.

Music: There's always the limbo, but to strike a real chord, warm up to the Red Hot Chili Peppers, Gypsy Kings, or Texas Tornados CDs.

Cactus Cooler

- Ice cubes
- 2 shots melon vodka, ***Skyy®***
- Splash melon liqueur, ***Midori®***

1. Fill a cocktail shaker with ice. Add ingredients and shake well.

2. Pour into two shot glasses. Makes 2 drinks.

Petite Lime Cheesecakes

- 1 package (8-ounce) cream cheese, softened, ***Philadelphia®***
- ½ cup sugar
- 3 tablespoons lime curd, ***Dickinson's®***
- 6 mini graham cracker crusts, ***Keebler®***
- Frozen whipped topping, thawed, ***Cool Whip®***
- Lime slices, for garnish
- Sugar, for garnish

1. In a medium mixing bowl, beat cream cheese and sugar with an electric mixer until creamy.

2. Beat in lime curd on low speed until just combined.

3. Spoon mixture into individual graham cracker crusts. Place on small baking sheet in freezer for 10 minutes.

4. Serve with a dollop of whipped topping and ¼ of a slice of lime that has been sprinkled with sugar. Make 6 servings.

Cosmorita

- Ice cubes
- 1 shot tequila, ***Jose Cuervo®***
- Splash lime juice, ***Rose's®***
- 2 shots cranberry juice, ***Ocean Spray®***
- Lime slice, for garnish

1. Fill a cocktail shaker with ice. Add tequila, lime juice, and cranberry juice. Shake several times.

2. Strain into a martini glass. Garnish with a lime slice. Makes 1 drink.

Sunny Shower Soirée

When life hands you lemons, there's only one thing to do: Throw a party! Lemon yellows abound in this uplifting gathering that blends the cheerful freshness of lemons, daisies, and daffodils with a lush green setting. Strokes of white, from the flowerpots to the napkins to the tablecloth, brighten the tablescape even more. Call on this lighthearted setting for the happiest of occasions: baby, wedding, or engagement showers; birthdays; or graduations—any time you want to summon up the sunniest of spirits. With the color scheme a natural, the rest is all about the grace notes. The napkins' delicate lacy edging is echoed in the etched glass of the lemonade canister and glass plates, the latticework on the compote and cake stand, and the filigree on the silver. From there, it's all about putting everything on stems and tiers and pedestals to add as much lift as you can. Even the chiffonlike cupcakes get a boost with a billowy swirl of frosting and a lemon drop on top. Carry the high spiritedness right through to the Triple Lemon Cake, with citrusy grilled chicken and luscious Lemon Tartlets rounding out the menu.

Food and Drink: A graceful glass canister filled with pink lemonade adds a rosy splash to the lemon theme. The pour spout lets guests help themselves—and its size means you won't squander precious party time refilling. Beside it, four sizes of etched glass plates stack into a tiered server, filled with store-bought lemon drops. Matching pedestals bearing Lemon Tartlets and a bowlful of fresh lemons complete the central food vignette. Cupcakes topped with lemon drops look luscious on a sweet serving tray that's really an ornate, white picture frame. Purchased lemon cookies look lovely on footed glass cake pedestals.

IZZE

Accent Pieces: Turn a fountain into a beautiful beverage bar that echoes the tiered food presentation on your serving table. (If you don't have a fountain, buy one at an outdoor or home supply store—you'll love it for a lifetime.) Fill the fountain basin with ice and decorate with bottles of lemony soft drinks and yellow Popsicles® that keep to the sun-splashed theme. Tuck in faux daisies and lemons—some whole, some halved—to add interest and fragrance.

Place Setting: Easy does it with a brunch buffet. Stow pretty faux pearl-handled silverware in whitewashed French flowerpots. Spray paint terra-cotta pots white and embellish with a daisy and wide sheer-and-yellow ribbon hot-glued around the top; daisy chain trim and a yellow satin ribbon bow around the other. Tucked inside, napkin ruffles mimic a tissue bouquet.

Centerpiece: A Cinderella carriage is a romantic plus. Buy a tabletop version in white (or spray paint it); bedeck it with hot-glued-on daisies, daffodils, and faux lemons. The invitation rests inside, framed in a tissue-wrapped box. Wrap the bottom of a shallow gift box in white tissue paper. Line the bottom with yellow paper cut to fit, overlaid with a same-size sheet of white latticed paper. Hot-glue a small, square sheet of green paper on top of and centered over a slightly larger sheet of the yellow paper to mimic frame matting. Hot-glue the invite on top and center it in the box. Embellish with a clipped daisy bloom and yellow and white ribbons. Park the carriage in the center of the buffet or at an entrance to let guests know this party's going to be a ball.

Pink Lemonade Wine Spritzers

1 can (12-ounce) frozen concentrated pink lemonade, *Minute Maid®*
1 bottle (750-ml) Chardonnay
3 cups lemon-lime soda, *Sprite®*
½ cup lemon vodka, *Absolut®*

1. In a large pitcher, combine all ingredients and stir. Refrigerate for 1 hour to blend flavors. Serve chilled. Makes 4 servings.

Menu Ideas: Purchase rice pilaf from your local deli; sprinkle with toasted almond slices. Serve alongside my Macaroni Salad and Lemon-Herb Butter-Basted Chicken.

Macaroni Salad

1 cup dried elbow or medium shell macaroni, *Barilla®*
½ cup dairy sour cream, *Knudson®*
¼ cup mayonnaise, *Hellman's®*
2 teaspoons Dijon mustard, *Grey Poupon®*
2 teaspoons milk
¼ teaspoon black pepper
½ cup chopped green bell pepper
2 tablespoons sliced green onion
¼ cup shredded cheddar cheese

1. Cook macaroni according to package directions. Drain well. Rinse with cold water; drain again.

2. In a bowl, stir together sour cream, mayonnaise, mustard, milk, and black pepper.

3. Stir the cooked macaroni, bell pepper, and green onion into the bowl. Toss lightly to coat. Gently stir in cheese. Cover and chill at least 3 hours and up to 24 hours. Before serving, stir in more milk, if necessary. Makes 6 servings.

Lemon-Herb Butter-Basted Chicken

1 stick butter, melted
1 tablespoon hollandaise sauce mix, *McCormick®*
2 teaspoons salt-free citrus herb seasoning, *Spice Island®*
2 tablespoons lemon juice, *ReaLemon®*
8 boneless, skinless chicken breasts, halved
Garlic salt, *Lawry's®*
Lemon-pepper seasoning, *Lawry's®*

1. Set up grill for direct cooking over medium heat. Oil grate when ready to start cooking.

2. In a small pan over medium heat, melt butter. Stir in sauce mix, citrus herb seasoning, and lemon juice. Cook 1 minute. Remove from heat; set aside.

3. Rinse chicken with cold water and pat dry. Season with garlic salt and lemon pepper.

4. Grill chicken on hot oiled grill 6 to 8 minutes per side or until done, basting with sauce every few minutes. Makes 8 servings.

Indoor method: Preheat broiler. Prepare chicken and basting sauce as directed. Place chicken on foil-lined baking sheet or broiler pan. Broil chicken for about 15 minutes per side, basting with butter sauce every 5 minutes.

Lemon Tartlets

2 **rolled refrigerated unbaked piecrusts, *Pillsbury*®**
1 **box (4.3-ounce) cook-and-serve lemon pudding mix, *Jell-O*®**
4 **egg yolks, slightly beaten**
¼ **cup sugar**
3 **cups lemonade, *Minute Maid*®**
2 **teaspoons finely grated lemon zest**
Lemon slices, for garnish (optional)

1. Preheat oven to 450 degrees F. Unroll piecrusts. Lay tartlet pans upside down on unrolled crusts; cut piecrust into circles around pans, leaving a 1-inch border. Press cutouts into pans. (Using 4½-inch tartlet pans, 2 tart shells can be cut from one crust. Gather scraps and reroll; cut out two more. Repeat with other crust.) Place tartlet shells on a sheet pan; bake for 10 to 12 minutes or until golden brown.

2. In a medium saucepan, whisk together pudding mix, egg yolks, sugar, and ½ cup of the lemonade until pudding mix dissolves. Stir in remaining lemonade and lemon zest. Bring mixture to boil over medium heat; cook about 10 minutes, stirring occasionally. Cool for 5 minutes, stirring occasionally. Evenly pour filling into shells. Cool in the refrigerator until set. If desired, garnish with lemon slices. Makes 8 servings.

Triple Lemon Cake

1 **box (18.25-ounce) white cake mix, *Betty Crocker*®**
1¼ **cups water**
⅓ **cup vegetable oil**
3 **eggs**
2 **teaspoons coconut extract, *McCormick*®**
2½ **cups sweetened coconut, divided**
2 **teaspoons lemon extract, *McCormick*®**
2 **cans (16 ounces each) creamy white frosting, *Betty Crocker® Rich & Creamy***
Yellow food coloring, *McCormick*®

1. Preheat oven to 350 degrees F. Butter and flour three 8-inch round cake pans.

2. Combine cake mix, water, oil, eggs, and coconut extract in a large bowl. Beat for 2 minutes or until well blended. Stir in ½ cup coconut. Divide batter evenly among pans.

3. Bake for 20 to 30 minutes or until toothpick inserted into centers of cakes comes out clean. Cool cakes in pans on cooling rack for 15 minutes. Invert cakes onto cooling racks; remove pans. Cool completely.

4. Meanwhile, stir 1 teaspoon of lemon extract into each can of lemon frosting. Add yellow food coloring to frosting, if desired. Place 1 cake layer on serving platter. Spread ⅔ cup frosting over cake layer on platter. Top with second cake layer. Spread another ⅔ cup frosting over top of cake layer. Top with remaining cake layer. Frost top and sides of cake with remaining frosting. Sprinkle remaining 2 cups of shredded coconut over top and onto sides of cake. Makes 12 servings.

Mother's Strawberry Lunch

Remember all the times she took your temperature with just her hand? Baked you cookies when you'd had a bad day? Bought you those jeans you just had to have? To show Mom how much you appreciate all she's done, another brooch just won't do. Instead, give her a gift she'll truly cherish: together-time with those she loves. Fresh and natural sets the tone—and the table—with a straight-from-the-garden palette that blends the blue of the sky with the shimmer of the sun. A family of dainty cobalt and yellow pottery accessories is a craft store find, but you could just as easily mix and match pieces for a cheerful effect. Homey red strawberries dot the tablescape—in the dessert, in baskets, and as the star of the berry-patch centerpiece. Kick off the party by clinking glasses of Passion Fruit Martinis that swing right into the color and mood of such an upbeat celebration. For dessert, a bit of bubbly is definitely in order. You could toast Mom's years of devotion with a glass of Champagne, but instead, use this festive sparkler to enhance a beautiful Champagne Parfait. Served in a fabulous flute, it's a sweet way to raise a glass to your guest of honor.

Place Settings: Lemony yellows and deep cobalt give painted pottery a French country air, enhanced by a white lattice design that adds winsome garden inspiration. Crisp white napkins are tied with thin yellow satin ribbons and accessorized with stems of freesia and sprigs of faux strawberries. For the table runner, snip a swath of silky sheering fabric that lets the sunny yellow of the tablecloth shine through. Its feminine blue scroll design plays perfectly off the dishes' painted-on scalloped border.

Centerpiece: A cluster of faux strawberries gives the arrangement a little sparkle; tuck in plenty of faux greenery and fruit blossoms to hint at a summery strawberry patch. The tall squared urn balances the table's frills to keep it unfussy.

Place Card Favors: For a homestyle favor, pick up some canning jars (as shown on following page) with a raised fruit-embossed design and fill with color-coordinated Peach Preserves. (You can buy them new or find them at flea markets.) For the topper, cut a square of yellow gingham cloth with pinking shears and hot-glue to the lid. Secure with a narrow blue satin ribbon. A plain vintage-style label makes it nicely nostalgic.

Accent Pieces: Beaded faux berries glisten in a cute ceramic basket that works in tandem with the centerpiece to bring the reds, yellows, and blues together. Its curvy shape and handle recall vintage berry baskets, but the pattern is a match to the dishes and vase.

Music: If "Cherish" comes to mind when you think of Mom, choose The Association's *Greatest Hits*, which includes that loving ballad. Or put on Doris Day's *Greatest Hits* for more reminiscing.

Champagne Parfaits

(Pictured on page 89)

1¼ cups extra-dry Champagne, divided, *Korbel*®
¼ cup honey, divided, *SueBee*®
1 package (16-ounce) frozen mixed berries, thawed, *Dole*®
3 teaspoons grated orange zest, divided
¼ cup fresh orange juice
1 package (12.5-ounce) silken extra-firm tofu, *Mori Nu*®
Fresh mint sprigs, for garnish (optional)

1. In a glass measuring cup, combine ½ cup of the Champagne and 2 tablespoons of the honey, stirring until honey is dissolved. In a small bowl, pour Champagne mixture over thawed berries. Stir 2 teaspoons of the orange zest and orange juice into berry mixture. Let stand at room temperature for 30 minutes to 1 hour.

2. For champagne sabayon, place remaining ¾ cup champagne into a blender. Add tofu, the remaining 2 tablespoons honey, and the remaining 1 teaspoon orange zest. Cover and blend on HIGH until smooth. Refrigerate until ready to serve.

3. To serve, layer berry mixture and Champagne sabayon among six champagne flutes. If desired, garnish with fresh mint. Makes 6 servings.

Peach Preserves

13 jars (10-ounce) peach preserves, *Smucker's*®
8 clean pint jars

1. Spoon 16 ounces (about 2 cups) of preserves into each clean pint jar. (You will have a few ounces leftover.) If desired, process in a boiling-water canner for 5 minutes. If you don't process, store jars in the refrigerator.

2. Top each jar with a piece of gingham fabric and tie with a ribbon. Makes 8 pints.

Passion Fruit Martini

1 shot citrus vodka, *Stoli*®
1 shot white cranberry juice, *Ocean Spray*®
1 shot passion fruit juice, *Ceres*®
½ shot orange liqueur, *Cointreau*®
Ice cubes
Orange slice or star fruit slice, for garnish

1. Combine all ingredients, except fruit garnish, in a martini shaker filled with ice. Shake and strain into a martini glass. Garnish with an orange or star fruit slice. Makes 1 drink.

Memorial Day Sea Buffet

When we think of the beach, our minds drift to the serenity of sea blues and greens. This start-of-summer feast travels a different road, relying on red to carry the tone. While blues are muted, reds are loud and clear—the blazing ball of fire as the sun sinks into ocean, the red-gold of lobster shells, the paprika-colored coral sunning on the reef. Red razzle-dazzles with decor and food splashed fresh from the ocean against a background of white. A coral-patterned fabric sets the stage for the red coral centerpieces to deliver the knockout punch. Food is the star of this show, with easy Halibut Salsa Tacos, Steamers, lobster, and crab headlining the seafood buffet, while a fruit-topped pound cake ends it with a rainbow of reds. A blended Watermelon Fizz cocktail is paradise served against a beachy backdrop, but it's just as summery at home. Sometimes the beauty of a tablescape is that it takes you where you could not otherwise go. If you find yourself landlocked, kick off summer in the backyard. Use this same setting to celebrate a birthday, anniversary, bon voyage, or any chance to savor fresh seafood—wherever you are.

Centerpiece: The table sizzles with dramatic red coral, mixed with rouge red tapers in clear glass candleholders. A large chunk of red coral dominates, flanked with pieces of white coral and a few taller reds. If you have trouble finding red coral (usually available at a pet supply store), buy faux pieces from a craft store and spray paint them red. **Accent Pieces:** Light a path to the table. Just fill crackled-glass hurricanes with sand, steady red pillar candles in each, and anchor them in the sand to start a path. Use the same hurricanes to bookend the table. These came with a shell-encrusted base, but plain glass ones will illuminate with the same effect. **Fashion:** A flirty eyelet dress—or a beach cover-up—in red-hot red keeps it short and simple. My niece Stephanie keeps cool in breezy white linen ruffles (see page 58).

Food and Drink: First up is Halibut Salsa Tacos, made spicy and fruity with peaches and allspice. For starters, Steamers rule. Lightly seasoned littleneck clams and mussels, served with crusty bread to sop up the broth, cozy up to presteamed lobster and crabs, with corn on the cob as a sweet side. For dessert, top purchased pound cake with fresh strawberries and peaches that serve up a riot of juicy reds. Watermelon Fizz cocktails are beachy beauties, served in tall, graceful hurricane glasses that echo the hurricane candles on the table and lining the path.

Accent Pieces: When you dine outdoors, it's easy to create the appearance of a dining room with breezy white sheering hung from bamboo poles stuck in the sand and loosely gathered then knotted to emulate curtains.

Music: Match red's uptempo with evocative music, such as *Avalon* by Roxy Music, or add an exotic note with some salsa or flamenco music.

Watermelon Fizz

2 cups seedless watermelon chunks, *Ready Pac*®
6 ounces club soda, *Schweppes*®
2 tablespoons limeade frozen concentrate, *Minute Maid*®
1 tablespoon fresh mint, chopped
10 ice cubes
2 shots melon vodka, *Skyy*®
1 tablespoon sugar
Whole strawberries, for garnish

1. Combine all ingredients in blender. Blend for 40 seconds. Pour into glasses. Garnish with strawberries. Makes 2 drinks.

Halibut Salsa Tacos

1 pound halibut
1 packet (1-ounce) hot taco seasoning, *Lawry's*®
2 cups mild chunky salsa, *Newman's Own*®
1 cup frozen peach slices, chopped and thawed, *Dole*®
1 teaspoon ground allspice, *McCormick*®
1 package (8-ounce) coleslaw mix, *Ready Pac*®
8 yellow corn tortillas, *Mission*®

1. Set up grill for direct cooking over medium heat. Oil grate when ready to start cooking.

2. Rub halibut with taco seasoning. Let cure for 30 minutes. Grill halibut 4 minutes per side, covered. Let cool. Cut into bite-size pieces.

3. In a medium-size bowl, combine salsa, peaches, and allspice.

4. Put halibut pieces in warm tortillas; cover with salsa and coleslaw. Serve warm. Make 4 servings.

Steamers

4 pounds fresh live littleneck clams, scrubbed
½ cup unsalted butter
2 leeks, cleaned and sliced, white and light green parts only
2 teaspoons salt-free seafood grill and broil, *Spice Hunter®*
½ teaspoon red pepper flakes, *McCormick®*
1 bottle (750-ml) Chardonnay
2 teaspoons crushed garlic, *Christopher Ranch®*
Crusty sourdough bread, for serving
2 pounds fresh live mussels, beards removed and scrubbed

1. At least 1 hour before cooking clams, soak clams in 1 gallon water to which ⅓ cup kosher salt and 1 cup cornmeal has been added. Do not use iodized salt; it will instantly kill the clams.

2. In a steamer or large pot, melt butter. Saute leeks until soft. Add remaining ingredients, except bread and seafood; bring to boil. Reduce heat to a simmer or slow boil and add clams and mussels. Cover with a tight-fitting lid and steam over low heat until clams and mussels have opened, about 5 to 10 minutes. Discard any clams or mussels that have not opened.

3. Transfer to serving bowls and ladle with broth. Serve hot with crusty bread to soak up broth. Makes 6 servings.

Place Card Favors: Seashell place cards add softness to bold place settings. Buy photo frames ready-made and slip name cards inside or hot-glue seashells on a white frame. Buy shells by the bag at craft stores or collect your own. **Place Settings:** Red can overwhelm a table, so use it sparingly but powerfully. Choose white plates with the barest hint of red at the rim, adding texture with the top plates' swirls. Finish by gathering white napkins and fastening them with a ponytail holder in the same shade. **Accent Pieces:** Give guests a warm welcome by lighting a path to the table with crackled glass shell hurricanes hosting red wax pillars.

Father's Day BBQ

Here's one for the road, an all-car classic that puts Dad in the driver's seat. Whether he's into a '60s Corvette or a '70s Mustang convertible, the fun-loving decor and hot-from-the-grill guy food celebrates man and his four-wheeled friends in all their shared glory. It's June—the gateway to summer—so take the party outdoors. Set a boyish tone with a red, white, and blue car-print tablecloth that's a flashback to the '20s, '30s, and '40s. Layers of primary colors rev up the party mood, with a red cotton runner headed lengthwise down the table, and green, yellow, and blue runners making horizontal tracks as makeshift place mats. Gas up the grill and get things cooking with Black Jack Lamb Rack, tender Grilled Asparagus, and smoky Bacon-Cheese Corn, served with striped highballs that are a blast from the past. It's a clever way to celebrate Dad's big day, spice up a backyard barbecue, or end a road trip party on a summer Sunday.

Centerpiece: A collection of model cars, showcased on steel storage bin pedestals, reflects the joy of boy toys. Raid the attic—or a boy's bedroom—for a set to borrow or pick them up at garage sales, thrift shops, or toy stores for a few dollars apiece. **Favors:** Comfort food confections brighten the table when displayed in red ceramic bowls and are just as good to go on their own in racy red boxes. Salty, yet sweet chocolate-covered pretzels, popcorn, and candy bark offer a medley of fun flavors (go to www.helpusa.org/comfortfoods).

Place Settings: White plates edged in cobalt pop against the rainbow of fabrics. To tap into the car mania, pull yellow and blue striped napkins through the elastic strings of retro red, blue, and yellow air fresheners.

Accent Pieces: Square vases of multicolor hydrangeas and ranunculus bookend the tablescape. Use silk flowers to keep your table fresh instead of flowers that wilt in the sun. High-octane accents, like red-banded tin gas cans, glint off the chrome storage boxes and silverware.

Place Cards: Personalized license plates turn miniature cars into keepsake place cards. Simply handwrite or computer type each guest's name on a rectangle of card stock and hot-glue it to the front of the car.

Music: The Beach Boys will make sure you have *"Fun, Fun, Fun,"* with or without the T-bird, or spin a compilation CD of retro favorites, like the B52's "*Love Shack*" and Roger Miller's "*King of the Road*."

Food: Hearty Black Jack Lamb will be sure to please dads with its grilled outside taste. Add a healthy touch with tender Grilled Asparagus and flavorful Bacon-Cheese Corn.

Fashion: What to wear? A sporty shirtdress in race car red matches your little red Corvette mood—and the table too.

Bacon-Cheese Corn

1 packet (1.5-ounce) four-cheese sauce mix, *Knorr®*
3 tablespoons mayonnaise, *Best Foods®*
4 ears corn on the cob, shucked and cleaned
4 slices thick-cut bacon, *Oscar Mayer®*

1. Set up grill for direct cooking over medium heat.

2. In a small bowl, thoroughly mix sauce packet and mayonnaise. Brush corn with mixture. Wrap with bacon slice and wrap in foil. Cook on hot grill for 25 to 30 minutes, turning often. Remove from grill; serve hot. Makes 4 servings.

Grilled Asparagus

1 pound asparagus spears, trimmed
2 tablespoons butter, melted
1 tablespoon snipped fresh dill
1 clove garlic, minced
¼ teaspoon black pepper
Parmesan cheese

1. Place asparagus in a grilling rack or in a large disposable foil pan. Drizzle with butter and sprinkle with dill, garlic, and pepper.

2. Grill asparagus directly over medium coals. Grill for 7 to 10 minutes or until asparagus is crisp-tender, stirring occasionally. (For a gas grill, preheat grill. Reduce heat to medium. Place foil pan on grill rack over heat. Cover and grill as above.) To serve, transfer asparagus to a serving dish. Sprinkle with Parmesan cheese. Makes 4 servings.

Black Jack Lamb Rack

1 cup whiskey, *Jack Daniel's®*
1 cup steak sauce, *Lea & Perrins®*
½ cup molasses, *Grandma's®*
2 racks of lamb
1 tablespoon garlic salt, *Lawry's®*
2 teaspoons black pepper

1. Set up grill for direct cooking over medium-high heat. Oil grate when ready to start cooking. In a small saucepan, combine whiskey, steak sauce, and molasses. Bring to boil and reduce to simmer for 20 minutes. Remove from heat; set aside.

2. Season racks of lamb with garlic salt and pepper. Grill racks on hot oiled grill, meat-sides down, for 10 to 12 minutes. Turn and baste meat with sauce every 5 minutes. Continue cooking for another 10 to 12 minutes.
Tip: If bones start to burn, fold a piece of aluminum foil over the ends.

3. Remove from grill and baste with sauce. Let stand 5 minutes before cutting. Serve cut chops with remaining sauce on the side. Makes 6 servings.

Pyramid

Labor Day Cookout

When autumn's just around the bend, say "Happy Trails" to summer with this chic Western-style picnic. Stripes and plaids tap into the beauty of the American West, from the sandy pinks of the desert to the splashy purples in the canyons to the golden-orange tinge of a spectacular sunset. Build from a tablecloth of burgundy ticking, topped with softer rose red and butterscotch plaid runners heading horizontally across the table to stand in for place mats. Brown glass bottles of beer, amber-hued cocktails, crusty breads, cheeses, and mini pinecones all add rough-hewn hues. Open up your country-chic chuck wagon and dish up juicy Tri-Tip Steak and smoky Mesquite Beans, served with deli salads and a deep-dish pie. Quench thirst in style with a posse of Plum-treenis, made with plum wine and vodka and served in glasses with metal stems. Count on it all to help you lasso a heaping helping of fun before fall begins or use its rustic reds and golds all autumn as a teaser to the holidays to come.

Accent Pieces: Big copper buckets are at home filled with iced-down beer. The Georgia O'Keeffe-style invitations use scrapbooking decals. Use paper cut-outs to create the desert backdrop on blank cards; complete by computer-printing the details on light paper. Cut them into mountain shapes and paste them in place. Rustle up cowboy accents such as a Stetson® boot and sheriff's badge and hot-glue in place.

Place Setting: A copper-color ceramic plate with ropelike edging and wooden-handled silverware carry a cattle-wrangling theme to the tabletop. Fold woven striped kitchen towels across the plates to serve as napkins and line up the utensils on top.

Centerpiece: Miniature wooden highback chairs tap into the cowboy color scheme, playing host to amber pillar candles that cast ambient lighting. To keep it neat—and safe—buy dripless candles and hot-glue them to the chairs to secure. Outdoorsy metal candle lanterns carry through on the bunkhouse theme (remember, citronella keeps bugs at bay).

Accent Pieces: Two wooden barrels—reminiscent of whiskey pouring freely in a Wild West saloon—are topped with a plank of wood for a makeshift sideboard. No barrels—no problem! You can use home store sawhorses for an equally thematic effect. Below the sideboard, I've put together my famous "beer-on-the-wall bench." That's right—I decorate with beer! And why not? The bottles have such fascinating, festive labels, they deserve showing off. Just line them up on a rustic bench to add a clever accent—and refreshment too.

Food and Drink: Wheel in a barrow full of corn chips in a clear acrylic wheelbarrow. The red chips match the sidecar of salsa—and the wine—for decorative effect. Make life simpler by choosing salsas that come in pretty jars. You won't need to bring an extra dish to the picnic—simply take off the label, open the jar, and serve. When it's empty, toss it in the trash. Continue the food-as-decor idea with textured ready-mades, such as cheese in the rind, crackers, a deep-dish country pie, and round breads and baguettes arranged in a chinos. Love that hi-ho silver effect!

Music: *Gunfighter Ballads* and *Trail Songs* by old-time favorite Marty Robbins will have everyone longing for the old frontier.

Plum-treeni

- Ice cubes
- 2½ ounces currant vodka, ***Absolut®***
- 1½ ounces plum wine, ***Gekkeikan®***
- Plums, sliced, for garnish (optional)

1. In a cocktail shaker filled with ice cubes, add vodka and plum wine. Shake. Strain into martini glass. If desired, garnish with plum slice. Makes 1 drink.

Tri-Tip Steak

- 2½ pounds tri-tip steak
- 2 packets (1.25 ounces each) original chili seasoning, ***McCormick®***
- 3 tablespoons granulated garlic, ***Spice Hunter®***
- 1 tablespoon kosher salt
- 1 tablespoon salt-free all-purpose seasoning, ***McCormick®***
- 2 tablespoons sugar
- 1 cup whiskey, ***Jack Daniel's®***
- ½ cup apple cider

1. Rinse steak and pat dry. Cover and pat tri-tip with chili seasoning, garlic, salt, all-purpose seasoning, and sugar. Place seasoned tri-tip in a large zip-top plastic bag; pour whiskey and cider over meat. Marinate in refrigerator for 1 to 3 hours.

2. Set up grill for direct cooking over medium-high heat. Oil grate when ready to start cooking.

3. Remove steak from refrigerator; let come to room temperature (approximately 20 to 30 minutes).

4. Remove steak from marinade; discard marinade. Place steak on hot oiled grill and cook 12 to 15 minutes per side for medium or until internal temperature reaches 145 degrees F to 150 degrees F. Transfer steak to a platter and let rest 5 to 10 minutes. Slice thinly across the grain and serve warm. Makes 4 servings.

Mesquite Beans

- 1 can (28-ounce) baked beans, ***Bush's®***
- 2 tablespoons spicy brown mustard, ***Gulden's®***
- ¼ cup Mesquite grilling sauce, ***McCormick® Grill Mates®***
- ¼ cup real bacon pieces, ***Hormel®***
- 5 slices center-cut bacon, (optional) ***Oscar Mayer®***

1. Set up grill for direct cooking over medium heat.

2. In a bowl, stir to combine beans, mustard, mesquite sauce, and bacon pieces. Pour bean mixture in a Dutch oven or 8-inch cast-iron skillet. If desired, cover beans with bacon slices.

3. Cook on covered grill for 30 minutes. Makes 4 servings.

Holidays

Beneath the turkey and the trimmings, the fruitcake, and all the tricks and treats, holidays are, at heart, a fusion of food, family, and friends. It's that gathering together around a table that brings us home and keeps us connected when life has flung us far apart.

As the years have passed, my holidays have ceased to be about buying the perfect present or baking that 20-ingredient recipe from scratch. Instead, they're about love, laughter, and simple foods shared with family and friends. Semi-Homemade® takes the pressure off with quick and easy recipes that help you set a festive table without spending days in the kitchen.

Since childhood, I've expressed love with food, and holidays give us the chance to celebrate the sentiment year-round. Ring in the New Year with a sparkle-draped setting, Crystal-Rum Cookies, and Shimmer-tinis. Take a break from all those Easter eggs with an Upside-Down Apple Skillet Pie and Butter-Rum Coffee, prettied up with pastels. Come July, it's time for red, white, and barbecue, starting with Cherry Coke® Ribs and a festive blue punch. Halloween wouldn't be Halloween without Bloodshot Eyecakes and a Vampire Kiss Martini. And a nutcracker table decked with Marmalade Meatballs and Ice Blue Snowflake Cocktails makes Christmas Cheer white—and blue.

The gift of friendship is always in season. Come simplify, savor, and celebrate—with Semi-Homemade®.

Christmas Cheer

Spread cheer to those on your holiday list with a yuletide party they'll look forward to for weeks and savor all season long. Capture the magic of the season with a toyland fantasy theme, led by a nutcracker brigade marching to the beat of the *Nutcracker Suite* ballet. A jaunty plaid tablecloth enlivens the table with Christmas colors, repeated in the reds and greens of the dinnerware and festive food accent pieces. Childlike place cards of red or green Christmas stockings are cut from construction paper. Just write guests' names on them and tuck them under Santa's sleigh, a party favor sure to tickle the little kid in everyone. (See directions on page 115.) Stack glass cake pedestals into a "treat yourself" buffet, piled high with glistening grapes, zesty cheese balls, assorted crackers, and sweet-treat cookies. Swirls of red satin ribbon, peppermints, and candy canes add decorative flair, and nutcrackers flank the stacked cake plates to create a colorful centerpiece. Candy canes add more color and do double duty as drink stirrers for minty Candy Cane Cocktails. Mix up a tray of Ice Blue Snowflake Cocktails or Gingerbread Martinis, ladle up some Marmalade Meatballs—everyone loves these—and you've got the recipe for the very best holiday ever.

Decorative Details: The Chief Commander Nutcracker holds an Ice Blue Snowflake Martini on top of a glass-bedecked tree. Made with colored craft resin and rimmed with hot glue and faux snow, the nutcracker's martini is a ringer for the real thing, above right. Dusted with coconut "snow," the cocktails coordinate with the white taper candlesticks that match the cocktail glass tree ornaments.

Candy Cane Cocktail

Ice cubes
1 shot vanilla rum, *Bacardi*®
1 shot white chocolate liqueur, *Godiva*®
1 shot peppermint schnapps, *DeKuyper*®
Candy cane, for garnish

1. Fill cocktail shaker with ice cubes. Add all ingredients, except candy cane garnish. Shake well and strain into martini glass. Garnish with a candy cane. Makes 1 drink.

Santa Sleigh Favors: You'll need: Graham crackers, white royal icing*, red royal icing*, sugar wafers, teddy bear cookies, red fruit roll-ups, Starbursts®, licorice vines, candy canes, shredded coconut, chocolate foil-wrapped Santa (unwrapped).

Sleigh bottom #1: Coat 1 side of a graham cracker cookie completely with white royal icing. Place 2 candy canes on top, keeping the hooks pointing upward; hold them in place for a few seconds to let set. Sprinkle coconut over the whole cracker and candy canes and set aside to let dry.

Sleigh bottom #2: Coat 1 side of another graham cracker completely with red royal icing and set aside to dry.

Presents: Pipe ribbons with white royal icing on Starbursts®.

Santa's seat: Take 2 sugar wafer bars (attached) and completely wrap with a fruit roll-up. Take another pair of wafers and do the same. Place seam sides down to keep them from unfolding. Set aside.

To assemble: Pipe a thin line of white royal icing over the length of the candy canes that are attached to sleigh bottom #1. Place sleigh bottom #2 (red graham cracker) on top of candy canes (red side up) and hold for a few seconds to let set. Make a seat out of the fruit roll-up covered sugar wafers by making an "L" shape on top of red cracker. Use one as the seat and the other as the back. On one side of the seat stack a few candy gifts; on the other side, place the chocolate Santa. Spread out 1 fruit roll-up and place a few gifts in the middle and make a pouch, tying the ends of the roll-up together with a licorice vine, like a beggar's purse. Place gift pouch behind Santa's seat and secure bottom to sleigh with royal icing.

****To make Royal Icing:*** In a large mixing bowl combine 3¼ cups powdered sugar, 3 tablespoons meringue powder, and ½ teaspoon cream of tartar. Add ½ cup warm water, and 1 teaspoon vanilla. Beat with an electric mixer on LOW speed until combined; beat on HIGH speed 7 to 10 minutes or until mixture is very stiff. If desired, tint with food coloring. Makes about 5 cups.

Tiered Cheeseballs

- **4 ounces blue cheese**
- **2 packages (8 ounces each) cream cheese, *Philadelphia*®**
- **1¼ cups finely chopped dried dates, *Dole*®**
- **Basil leaves**

1. In a food processor fitted with a metal blade, combine blue cheese and cream cheese. Process until smooth. Transfer to an airtight container and chill in refrigerator for at least 4 hours.

2. Once chilled, form cheese mixture into 6 even balls. Roll each ball into chopped dates. Arrange cheeseballs on tiered platter. Garnish with fresh basil leaves. Makes 6 cheeseballs.

Ice Blue Snowflake Cocktail

(Pictured on page 113)

- **1 shot vodka, *Blue Ice*®**
- **1 shot liqueur, *Envy*®**
- **½ shot orange liqueur, *Cointreau*®**
- **1 cup ice cubes**
- **Sweetened shredded coconut,* for garnish**

1. Add all ingredients, except coconut garnish, to blender and blend on HIGH until smooth.

2. Pour into martini glasses dipped into sweetened shredded coconut. Makes 1 drink.

***Tip**: To make coconut stick to glass, dip rim in honey or corn syrup.

Food and Drink: Stacked glass cake pedestals are piled high with glistening grapes, cheeseballs, crackers, and cookies accented with peppermints and swirls of red ribbon. Candy canes double as drink stirrers for Candy Cane Cocktails—a minty counterpoint to Marmalade Meatballs. Gingerbread Martinis sport an iced-cookie garnish.

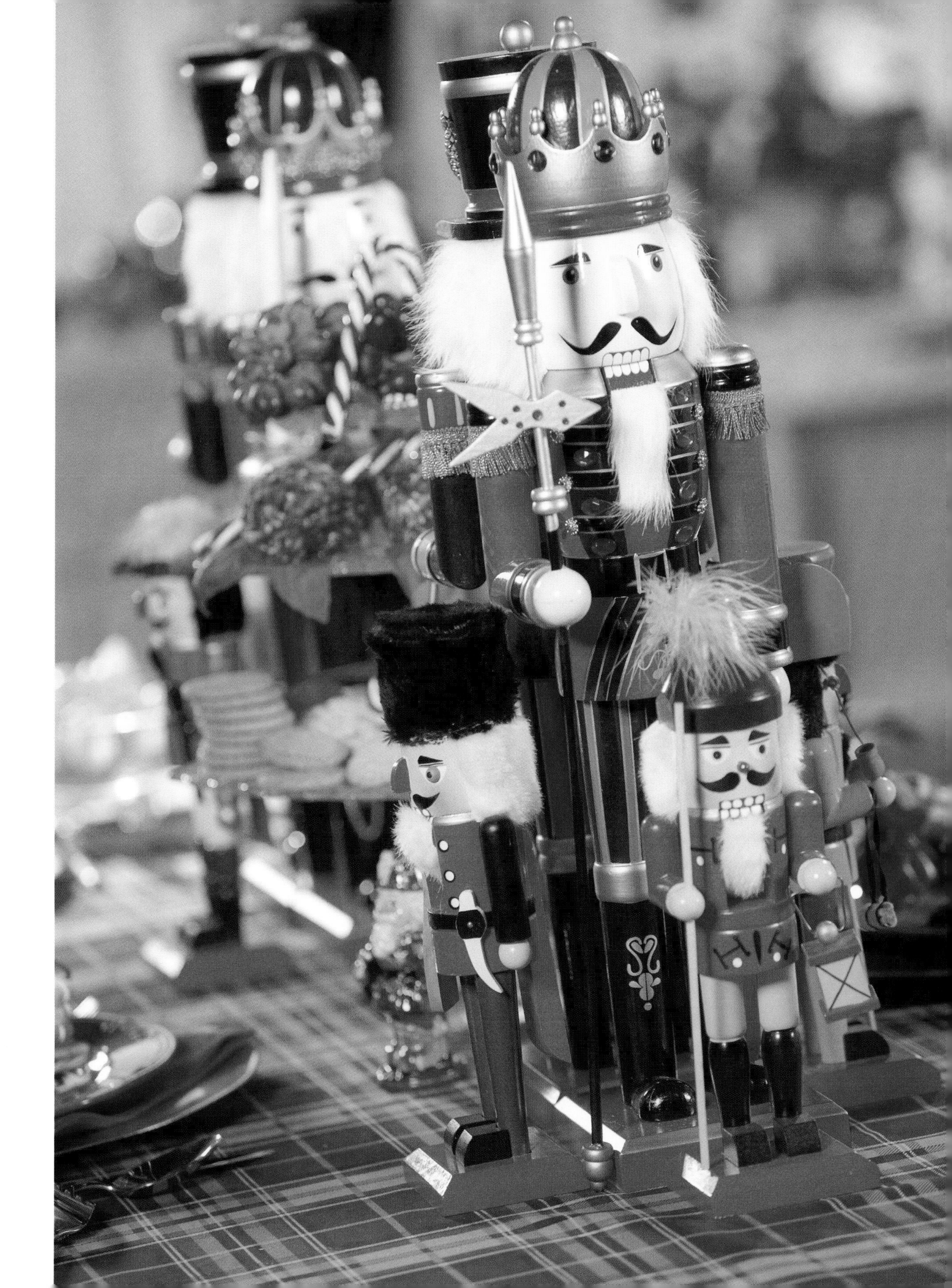

Gingerbread Martini

- 1 shot vanilla vodka, *Stoli®*
- 1 shot hazelnut liqueur, *Frangelico®*
- ½ shot butterscotch schnapps, *DeKuyper®*
- Ice cubes
- 4 ounces ginger beer, *Reed's®*
- Dark rum, *Myer's®*
- Gingerbread man cookie, *Pepperidge Farm®*, for garnish

1. Pour vodka, hazelnut liqueur, and butterscotch schnapps into a cocktail shaker filled with ice. Shake well. Strain into high ball glass or any 8 ounce glass filled with ice. Top with ginger beer. Add dark rum. Garnish with gingerbread man. Makes 1 drink.

Marmalade Meatballs

- 2 pounds fully cooked frozen meatballs, *Armanino®*
- 1 bottle (16-ounce) Catalina salad dressing, *Kraft®*
- 1 cup orange marmalade, *Smucker's®*
- 3 tablespoons Worcestershire sauce, *Lea & Perrins®*
- ¾ teaspoon red pepper flakes, *McCormick®*
- Butterhead lettuce leaves, for garnish

1. Place frozen meatballs in a 5-quart slow cooker.

2. In a medium bowl, stir together salad dressing, marmalade, Worcestershire sauce, and red pepper flakes. Pour over meatballs, stirring to coat.

3. Cover and cook on HIGH heat setting for 2 to 3 hours. Line a serving bowl with lettuce leaves; fill with meatballs and some of the sauce. Makes 16 servings.

John
Rich

A Thoughtful Thanksgiving

Thanksgiving is all about being thankful and thoughtful. When you carry a theme from the door to the table, that attention to detail sets you apart and shows your guests just how special you think they are. The holidays are hectic, true, but you can still pull off a gracious gathering with minimal fuss. Simply pick a theme—the colors of the harvest come naturally now—and purchase products that bring home the look: a fiery leaf-and-pinecone wreath, faux fall flowers, and candles in reds, golds, and browns all add to the warm, welcoming setting. Say the rest with food. A kickoff cocktail spreads warmth—to all the senses—so start things off with a Hot Apple Toddy that smells as wonderful as it sips. The main table is resplendent in a neutral tablecloth spiced up with mini pecan-pumpkin pie place cards and orange-glazed Bundt cake bouquets that double as centerpieces. Bowls of tangerines, whole fruits, and nuts carry the rich brown-orange colors to sideboards and hall tables. Add family and friends and you've got the recipe for a thankful day.

Centerpiece: Prepare the Mini Bundt Cakes on page 124 or buy one large premade bundt cake from the store. To either, add a drippy, orange glaze and small rose and fruit nosegay toppers, and they're good to go. **Place setting:** Build on the neutral tablecloth with burnished brown chargers topped with earth-tone plates and softer-than-rust color napkins. Fall leaves and berries twirl up the stems of goblets, adding deeper notes of color to the Hot Apple Toddies.

Rich

Place Cards: Place cards, gift cards—they're one and the same. Dig into scrapbooking supplies for decorative medallions or paper cutouts that can be personalized with guests' names. Stand one in a ready-made pecan-pumpkin pie for a place card that's a sweet treat in more ways than one.

Favors: Tie up autumn-hued treats—such as brown chocolate cookies and golden-yellow dried apricots—in clear cellophane bags and wrap them with berry-ornamented wire. Pile them on a side table or a tray by the door to spread hospitality throughout the house.

Accent Pieces: Welcome guests to your home with a purchased wreath bursting with colorful autumn leaves and pinecones. Coordinate decor inside and out by hanging the wreath with the same wide coppery orange ribbon that ties the fabric to the dining chairs.

Chances are, you'll have more guests than you have dining room chairs. Recruit extra chairs from all over the house and make them a match with no-sew chair slips that unify the tablescape. Simply use a table runner, found fabric, or leftover yardage that's folded and secured with wired ribbon or a decorative cord tied into a bow. Here a textured tapestry pattern and a wide coppery satin ribbon unite the chairs and the table.

Silk leaf-adorned pheasants fly in a festive flair and add a grand finale finish.

Hot Apple Toddies

- 3 cups apple cider, *Martinelli's®*
- 4 cinnamon sticks, *McCormick®*
- ½ cup spiced rum, *Captain Morgan®*
- ½ cup cinnamon schnapps, *Goldschlagger®*
- Cinnamon sticks, for garnish*, *McCormick®*

1. In a medium saucepan over medium heat or in a 4-quart slow cooker, combine all ingredients and heat through. Do not boil. Mull for 45 to 60 minutes.

2. Serve warm in footed glasses garnished with cinnamon stick swizzles. Makes 4 drinks.

*Note: If using bittersweet to garnish food items, make sure it is faux.

Mini Bundt Cakes

Cakes

- Nonstick cooking spray, *Pam®*
- 1 box (18.25-ounce) lemon cake mix, *Betty Crocker® Super Moist*
- 1 box (3.4-ounce) lemon instant pudding and pie filling, *Jell-O®*
- 1¼ cups water
- ⅓ cup vegetable oil
- 3 eggs

Glaze

- 2 cups powdered sugar, sifted
- 1 cup lemon curd, stirred to loosen, *Dickinson's®*
- ¼ cup water
- Orange food coloring, (optional) *McCormick®*

1. For the cakes, preheat oven to 350 degrees F. Lightly spray 12 mini Bundt cake pans or 1 large Bundt cake pan with cooking spray; set aside. In large bowl, combine cake mix, pudding mix, water, oil, and eggs. Beat with an electric mixer for 2 minutes. Divide batter among prepared mini Bundt pans (or pour all into large Bundt pan).

2. Bake mini Bundt cakes for 30 minutes (large Bundt cake for 35 minutes) or until toothpick inserted in centers comes out clean. Cool cakes in pans for 15 minutes. Invert cakes onto a cooling rack; remove pans and cool. Trim stems of nosegay so that it fits into center of cake without falling over. Remove nosegays; set aside.

3. For the glaze, in saucepan, whisk together all glaze ingredients, except food coloring. Simmer for 10 minutes over low heat, stirring frequently. If desired, stir food coloring into glaze. Cool slightly; drizzle over Bundt cake. Allow icing to set (about 20 minutes). Place premade fall nosegays into centers of cakes; adorn base of cake pedestal with faux leaves. Remove nosegays and leaves before serving. Makes 12 mini cakes or 1 large cake.

Harvest Pilgrimage

As the fall leaves turn, our thoughts turn, too, to the upcoming holidays and the most American feast of all—Thanksgiving dinner. Thanksgiving is all about showing appreciation for the food the land gives us and the people we share it with. Subtlety and richness are the keys to this bountiful theme with colors drawn from the fruits of the harvest. Start with a table covering embossed with browns and golds. Use pinking shears to create a no-hem table covering from an inexpensive fabric remnant. Berry topiaries add a cornucopia of color, while carved wooden Pilgrims and Indians alongside resin turkeys are rustic reminders of the first Thanksgiving. For a twist on the traditional pumpkin pie, try my Sweet Potato Coconut Cake, set on a pedestal and adorned with dried wheat stalks and leaves around the base. Put on an instrumental CD, pour each guest a vibrant Burgundy Bubbler, and raise your glasses in gratitude for a memorable meal.

Place Settings: Layering a translucent glass plate over a metal leaf-shape charger makes decorative tableware food safe. Pale yellow napkins dress it up.

Place Cards: Gather fall leaves or cut faux leaves out of light and dark shades of textured paper. Write guests' names on the light leaf with a metallic pen, fit the two leaves together, and hole-punch the tops. Tie to the place setting with wired raffia wrapped around a pencil to create a corkscrew effect.

Favors: The cunning harvest box can hold recipes, keys, or trinkets. Cover the bottom with natural linen and the top with tablecloth fabric; glue wheat stalks around the base and top with plastic pumpkins and gords.

Accent Pieces: Cream-color ceramic pumpkins harmonize with the carved figures and the soft yellow napkins.

Burgundy Bubbler

1½ cups orange juice, chilled, ***Minute Maid®***
3 cups Burgundy wine or any leftover red wine, chilled
3 cups sparkling cider, chilled, ***Martinelli's®***

1. Pour ¼ cup orange juice and ½ cup red wine into each highball glass. Top off each with a ½ cup of sparkling cider. Serve chilled. Makes 6 servings.

Sweet Potato Coconut Cake

Butter-flavor nonstick cooking spray, *Pam®*
1 box (18.25-ounce) spice cake mix, *Betty Crocker®*
2 cups leftover mashed candied sweet potatoes or yams
3 eggs
1 teaspoon coconut extract, *McCormick®*
1¼ cups evaporated milk, *Carnation®*
¼ cup vegetable oil
2 cans (12 ounces each) whipped cream cheese frosting, *Betty Crocker®*
1½ teaspoons rum extract, *McCormick®*
¾ cup leftover cranberry sauce, drained, if necessary
2½ cups shredded coconut, *Baker's®*

1. Preheat oven to 350 degrees F. Lightly spray two 8- or 9-inch round cake pans with butter-flavor cooking spray; set aside.

2. In a large mixing bowl, combine cake mix, mashed sweet potatoes, eggs, coconut extract, evaporated milk, and oil. Use an electric mixer to beat on low speed for 30 seconds. Scrape down sides of bowl and beat for 2 minutes on medium speed. Divide batter between prepared cake pans. Bake in preheated oven for 45 to 55 minutes or until a toothpick inserted in centers of cakes comes out clean.

3. Let cakes cool in pan for 10 minutes. Invert onto a wire cooling rack to cool completely.

4. In a medium mixing bowl, combine frosting and rum extract; set aside.

5. Place one of the cooled cake layers on serving plate. Cut a triangle from the bottom corner of a small zip-top plastic bag. Spoon ¼ cup of frosting into bag and secure top with one hand. Use other hand to guide bag and squeeze a thick border of frosting around the edge of the cake layer. Spoon cranberry sauce in the center of frosting border. Carefully place the other cake layer on top.

6. Frost cake with remaining frosting. Sprinkle with coconut and gently pat to adhere to frosting. Slice and serve. Makes 12 servings.

HAPPY HALLO

Haute Halloween

Bubble, bubble, banish trouble—scare up treats on the double. I'll show you how! Blacken the mood by costuming your table in a tonal check black tablecloth and orange runner, teamed with hanging flag banners in striped and checkerboard patterns used as place mats. Halloween is the holiday where you can let your imagination run wild, not just in creating the tablescape but in conjuring up a masterful menu too. Stir up some truly gruesome goodies—Bloodshot Eyecakes and Ghoulish Pies are a scream as haute cuisine. Make your party a graveyard smash with a *Monster Mash* CD. Greet guests with a kiss—a Vampire Kiss Martini, that is. Create killer treats by securing Halloween candle buckets into a "pick one" pyramid and tying individual portions of candy into beribboned bundles that masquerade as the centerpiece. Set a wonderfully wicked table with bats and cats and witches, then transform a spooky black raven into a serving tray for scary but delicious treats. This party is such a scream, you might want to think of hosting one every year.

Fashion: Be a diva like Streisand or Liza with a Z. Don a feathered headdress and shimmy like Cher—or pretend you're a princess of pop like Madonna. I took a turn as all four and had a ball playing dress up—check out those most wicked wigs!

Vampire Kiss Martini

1 part raspberry liqueur, ***Chambord®***
1 part vodka, ***Absolut®***
1 part Champagne, ***Korbel®***
Wax teeth, candy corn, licorice, and/or blood orange slice, for garnish

1. Layer raspberry liqueur, vodka, and Champagne in a fluted or martini glass. Garnish with wax teeth, candy corn, licorice, and/or blood orange slice. Makes 1 drink.

Place Settings: Set a wicked table with dishes bearing bats and cats and witches—oh, my!—layered on orange napkins folded across black chargers.

Centerpiece: Make this killer table illuminate by stacking candle buckets into a pyramid. For accent pieces, glue a piece of crafts foam into the bottom of a bucket. Slide Gummy Worms, Trolli®, soft candies, and Lifesaver® eyeballs onto bent metal skewers and anchor them in the foam. Fill each box with candy to hide the foam.

Accent Pieces: Stuffed with holiday lights, resin pumpkins cast an eerie glow to the entry. Spook up your pantry with huge black spiderwebs and a recipe box covered with black and orange fabric, embellished with scrapbooking decals.

Candy Place Card Favors: Bundles of candy masquerade as place cards. Center a handful of candy on a sheet of cellophane and tie the cellophane with a black-and-white striped ribbon. Use a cookie cutter to trace a bat shape onto black paper, cut it out, and print the guest's name in gold. Hole punch the top and thread the ribbon through.

Bloodshot Eyecakes

Cupcakes
- 1 box (18.25-ounce) dark chocolate cake mix, *Betty Crocker®*
- 1⅓ cups chocolate milk
- ½ cup canola oil
- 3 eggs

Filling
- 1 box (3.4-ounce) instant butterscotch pudding, *Jell-O®*
- 1¼ cups milk
- ½ cup smooth peanut butter, *Skippy®*
- 1 container (12-ounce) ready-to-spread white frosting, *Betty Crocker® Creamy Deluxe®*
- Edible red decorating gel
- Plastic eyeballs

1. Preheat oven to 350 degrees F. Line twenty-four 2½-inch muffin cups with cupcake papers; set aside. In a large bowl, use a hand held electric mixer to beat together cake mix, chocolate milk, oil, and eggs on low speed for 30 seconds. Scrape sides of bowl with a rubber spatula and beat for 1 minute more on medium speed.

2. Use a ladle to fill each lined cupcake cup ⅔ full. Bake in preheated oven for 21 to 26 minutes or until toothpick inserted in the centers comes out clean.

3. Place on wire rack; let cool completely before filling and frosting, about 30 minutes.

4. For filling, combine pudding mix, milk, and peanut butter in a bowl. Whisk for 2 minutes until smooth and thickened. Refrigerate for 30 minutes. Spoon filling into a pastry bag fitted with a medium plain tip. Fill cupcakes by inserting tip into tops of cupcakes and squeezing a couple of tablespoons of filling into each. Spread 2 tablespoons frosting on each cupcake top.

5. Using red gel frosting, draw squiggly lines on the frosted cupcakes so that they look like veins. Place a plastic eyeball in the center of each cupcake. Makes 24 cupcakes.

Ghoulish Pies

- 4 containers (3.5 ounces each) vanilla pudding, *Jell-O®*
- Green food coloring, *McCormick®*
- 4 individual graham cracker pie shells, *Keebler®*
- 4 egg whites, room temperature
- Juice of ½ lemon
- Pinch of salt
- ½ cup sugar

1. Combine 4 pudding servings in bowl. Stir in green food coloring to desired color. Spoon green pudding into individual pie shells and refrigerate.

2. Beat egg whites, lemon juice, and pinch of salt. Slowly add sugar while beating. Beat on medium until stiff peaks form.

3. Remove pies from refrigerator. Top each pie with a spoonful of meringue. Frost with butter knife to form peaks. Toast top of meringue with a brûlée torch. Makes 4 pies.

Decorative Details: Turn a craft store raven into a serving tray. Choose a bird with sturdy legs and hot-glue a plate of Ghoulish Cream Pies on its back.

A Fabulous Fourth

Memorial Day, Flag Day, the Fourth of July—summer offers ample opportunities to fly America's favorite colors. Keep it supersimple with plates, tablecloths, and cutlery in a parade of patriotic hues. Better yet, make it all disposable—with sparklers to light and fireworks to watch, this is no night for doing dishes. Spread a white cloth over the table and flutter a flag banner around the rim with hook-and-loop tape (or use tacks to attach individual flags). Large red and blue check tea towels make dandy napkins—their size will be a plus with all that hands-on food. Forget standing on ceremony! Tote along a tub of iced soft drinks and fill flowerpots with red-color candies so guests can help themselves. Only an all-American menu will do, so fire up the grill and feast on Black Pepper-Crusted Burgers, Cherry Coke® Ribs, and Bourbon Beans with a colorful Strawberry-Pineapple Shortcake for dessert. Dip into a bowl of pool blue punch and toast three cheers for the red, white, and blue—and a quick cleanup too!

Centerpiece: A glass punch bowl makes a showy centerpiece. Fill with your favorite lemon-lime soda-Kool-Aid® punch recipe and ice. Use food coloring to achieve that cool blue hue. **Favors:** White spray paint turns plain terra-cotta pots into cute candy dishes—just fill with old-fashion dime-store candies, like red Jordan almonds, Red Hots®, or red licorice bites for fun take-aways.

Place Settings: Stack paper plates in a trio of sizes, shades, and designs at each seat. Keep plastic utensils in the same patriotic palette. **Accent Pieces:** Votive candles add another spark of red, eliciting oohs and aahs come dusk. Add pizzazz to the punch by slipping a large silver sparkler ornament into the punch bowl; attach mini sparklers to drink straws to reinforce the theme. Clear plastic goblets are downright spiffy these days, so take advantage and keep the picnic worry-free. For easy access, set up a tailgate beverage bar right out of the back of a red pickup. Your own backyard keeps it convenient, or snag a gazebo in a nearby park and have a grand old time. **Music:** Slip in *Ray Charles Sings for America* and *This Land Is Your Land: Songs of Freedom*, a compilation by various artists.

Cherry Coke® Ribs

2 full racks baby back ribs, quartered
3 cups beef broth, *Swanson*®
1 cup cherry cola, *Coca Cola*®
Water
1½ cups barbecue sauce, *Bull's Eye Original*®
1 cup honey, *SueBee*®
½ cup cherry cola, *Coca Cola*®

1. Place ribs, beef broth, and 1 cup of the cherry cola in a large heavy pot or Dutch oven. Add enough water to fully cover ribs. Bring to a boil. Reduce heat to low and simmer about 1 hour, or until tender. Remove ribs from pot; set aside.

2. Preheat grill for medium direct heat. In a medium bowl, combine barbecue sauce, honey, and cherry cola. Baste ribs generously with sauce. Grill ribs, uncovered, for about 4 minutes per side, or until desired doneness. Makes 4 servings.

Bourbon Beans

2 cans (16 ounces each) baked beans, drained, *Bush's*®
½ cup chili sauce, *Heinz*®
¼ cup real bacon pieces, *Hormel*®
¼ cup bourbon, *Jim Beam*®
2 tablespoons packed brown sugar
1 tablespoon molasses, *Grandma's*®

1. In medium saucepan, over medium-high heat, combine baked beans, chili sauce, bacon, bourbon, brown sugar, and molasses. Bring to a boil; reduce heat to medium. Cook for 10 minutes. Serve hot. Makes 4 servings.

Black Pepper-Crusted Burgers

Cognac-Mustard Sauce
- **½ cup cognac, *Hennessy*® or apple cider**
- **½ cup Dijon mustard, *Grey Poupon*®**
- **2 teaspoons fresh tarragon**

Burgers
- **1½ pounds ground sirloin**
- **2 packages (2 ounces each) onion soup mix, *Lipton*®**
- **¼ cup cognac, *Hennessy*®**
- **½ cup cracked black pepper, *McCormick*®**
- **Kaiser rolls**
- **Lettuce, tomato, red onion**

1. For Cognac-Mustard Sauce, in a small saucepan over medium-high heat, bring cognac to a boil and reduce by half, about 4 to 5 minutes. Remove from heat and let cool. Once cognac reduction has cooled, add to small bowl along with mustard and tarragon. Stir to combine; set aside.

2. Set up grill for direct cooking over high heat. Oil grate when ready to start cooking.

3. For burgers, in a mixing bowl, stir to combine ground sirloin, onion soup mix, and cognac. Wet your hands to prevent sticking and form into 4 patties slightly larger than rolls; set aside. Spread cracked pepper on a plate. Carefully press both sides of burgers into cracked pepper; set aside, covered in plastic wrap, and refrigerate if not cooking immediately.

4. Place burgers on hot oiled grill and cook 4 to 5 minutes per side for medium.

5. Serve hot on toasted kaiser roll with lettuce, tomato, onion, and a spoonful of sauce. Makes 4 servings.

Indoor method: Preheat oven to 400 degrees F. Prepare burgers as directed. Place burgers on wire rack over foil-lined baking sheet. Roast in preheated oven for 19 to 20 minutes or until internal temperature reaches 145 degrees F.

Strawberry-Pineapple Shortcake

- **1 container (14-ounce) frozen sweetened, sliced strawberries, thawed, *Dole*®**
- **2 cans (8 ounces each) pineapple chunks, drained, *Dole*®**
- **½ cup orange marmalade, *Knott's Berry Farm*®**
- **1 frozen pound cake (16-ounce), thawed, *Sara Lee*®**
- **1 container (8-ounce) strawberry cream cheese, *Philadelphia*®**
- **Pressurized whipped topping, for garnish**
- **Sprigs of mint, for garnish**

1. In a medium bowl, stir together strawberries, pineapple, and marmalade; set aside.

2. Slice thawed pound cake into 16 slices. Spread half of the slices with cream cheese. Set on serving plate. Spoon half of strawberry mixture over pound cake slices. Top with remaining pound cake slices and strawberry mixture.

3. Serve garnished with whipped cream and a sprig of mint. Makes 8 servings.

Maypole Parade

With spring come sunny skies and bright flowers that whisper of the summer ahead. What a great excuse for a party! Celebrate the season at its full-bloom best with a carefree gathering that offers a cheery backdrop for a child's birthday, a grammar-school graduation, or an anytime way to say, "I love spring!" Really, the whole season is cause for celebration from May Day on, so invite all your friends—and their children too—to eat, drink, and make merry. May Day is the height of spring, so it's only fitting that a maypole theme take the table to heights of fun. The rainbow, multicolored ribbons of a traditional maypole capture the shades of spring—pinks, reds, oranges, greens, blues, and yellows—and repeat them throughout the tablescape. Bright pastel stripes wave down the tablecloth like streamers in the breeze, connecting a carousel of cupcakes on either end. The food sashays right into the mood. Quick-and-easy Herb Pasta Salad wears party colors, cucumber-salmon tea sandwiches are shaped like daisies, and pretty-as-can-be Maypole Punch is dressed up with a fruity ice ring. Even the flowers on the cake are edible!

Place Settings: Spirited dinnerware stack in a colorful place setting that starts with a hot pink charger and pyramids ribbon-striped plates and a cookie place card. The streamer stripes on the cone-folded napkins match the tablecloth. Just fold napkins into triangles, set silverware on top, fold the side points, and fasten with mini clothespins. **Place Cards:** Cookie place cards are a hit with kids of all ages. Use several shades of piped icing to decorate them.

Food and Drink: A fruit-filled ice ring made in a Bundt pan keeps the Maypole Punch as fresh as the day outside. Served in stemmed sundae glasses, it's as festive as can be. Daisy-shape tea sandwiches make good-for-you fun food. Sandwich crisp cucumbers between slices of white bread and use a cookie cutter to cut into daisies. Top with piped salmon mousse—cream together canned salmon and mayonnaise and flavor it with dill.

Favors: Ring around the posies! Instead of May baskets, give everyone May cones. Just wrap lacy pastel doilies into paper cones and fill with bunches of soft-color faux flowers. If using real flowers, keep them fresh by triple-wrapping the stems in wet paper towels, plastic wrap, and aluminum foil before tucking the bouquet inside the doily cone.

Accent Pieces: Even cupcakes get their turn dancing around the maypole. To make this clever merry-go-round spin, turn a brightly colored bowl or flowerpot upside down, set a lazy Susan on top, and top it with a clear platter. Secure all with Tacky Wax®. The maypole is a paper towel dispenser with an acrylic disk from the hardware store placed at its base and decorated with hot-glued flowers and wrapped in ribbon. Bakery cupcakes are similarly garnished, but with edible flowers here.

Fashion: A fun smocked top in springy stripes echoes all those glorious maypole ribbons.

Accent Pieces: It's true—not many people have a maypole in the backyard. You can always make one by wrapping a purchased flag pole with long, wide streamers and setting a flowerpot on top. Tufts of store-bought cotton candy are served in colorful sugar ice cream cones. Cut holes in a piece of foam and tuck the cones through to give it a creatively classic carnival presentation.

Centerpiece: A prettied-up bakery cake becomes the queen of the May day celebration. Start with a white two-layer cake with pale green and pink frosting piped around its base. Top with store-bought cupcakes and a sprinkling of edible flowers. To make the flowers even sweeter, give them a light brushing of flavored syrup, then sprinkle with superfine sugar. The maypole is simply a child's magic wand that comes with ribbons attached. Hot-glue a faux flower or two on the tip and stand it upright in the center of the cake. If your cake stand has lattice edges, all the better—you can stream the ribbons through the loops to hold them in place.

Music: The lyrical piano melodies of George Winston's *Winter into Spring* fit with the carousel. Slip in Disney's *Springtime Favorites* by various artists for the kids.

Maypole Punch

1 cup frozen peach slices, ***Dole®***
1 cup frozen whole strawberries, ***Dole®***
¼ cup fresh mint leaves
1 can (46-ounce) pineapple juice, divided, ***Dole®***
½ cup frozen orange juice concentrate, ***Minute Maid®***
2 cups frozen sliced strawberries, thawed, ***Dole®***
2 cans (11.5 ounces each) peach nectar, ***Kern's®***
4 cups lemon-lime soda, ***Sprite®***
Extra-dry Champagne, *Korbel®*, for adults

1. Arrange a double layer of peaches, strawberries, and mint leaves in the bottom of a Bundt pan. Add enough pineapple juice to cover fruit. Freeze for at least 2 hours or until set.

2. In a large punch bowl, combine remaining ingredients, except Champagne. Stir to mix thoroughly.

3. To serve, remove Bundt pan from freezer. Unmold ice ring* and float in center of punch bowl. Ladle into glasses. For adults, top punch with Champagne. Makes 24 servings.

***Tip:** If ice mold is hard to remove, place Bundt pan in a warm water bath for 1 to 2 seconds; then unmold.

Herb Pasta Salad

1 package (8-ounce) haricots verts, ***Earth Exotics®***
1 box (12-ounce) tri-color rotini pasta, ***Barilla®***
1 jar (12-ounce) roasted yellow bell peppers, cut into small strips, ***Delallo®***
1 jar (12-ounce) roasted red bell peppers, cut into small strips, ***Delallo®***
½ cup mixed fresh herbs, such as mint, basil, tarragon, marjoram, chopped
¾ cup poppy seed salad dressing, ***Knott's Berry Farm®***
Edible flowers, for garnish

1. Bring a large pot of water to a boil. Add haricot verts and blanch for 3 minutes. Use a slotted spoon to remove and immerse in a bowl of ice water to stop cooking. Return pot of water to a boil.

2. Add pasta and cook for 8 minutes or until al dente. Drain pasta and let cool.

3. In a large serving bowl, combine all ingredients, except edible flowers. Toss until ingredients are thoroughly coated with dressing.

4. Garnish with edible flowers and serve cold or at room temperature. Makes 10 servings.

An Easter Treat

Easter is a time of renewal—in spirit and on the calendar. Flowers pop up, baby birds hatch, bunnies hip and hop, and the whole world wears its Sunday best. Bring that outside beauty in, starting with whimsical Victorian-style birdhouses clustered into an Easter village proudly displayed on your buffet table. A pastel plaid tablecloth (or simply a piece of unhemmed fabric) picks up the hues in the cotton candy-tone roofs and are revisited in the napkins. The fluted plates and gold-trimmed teacups with triangular saucers boast four colors and modern designs. Bright-colored eggs are hidden on the table in tea cups turned egg cups, in greenery-wrapped birds' nests, and in mossy twig baskets. The food is as lovely as the table. An Upside-Down Apple Skillet Pie glows with a golden apple glaze. Serve Butter-Rum Coffee—a blend of butterscotch, vanilla, and whipped cream—for a sweet celebration of new beginnings.

Centerpiece: This charming tabletop vignette pairs a grapevine basket and birds' nests into a stand-alone centerpiece that can be doubled to become endpieces to the buffet. Just line the bottom of a twig basket with dried moss and build height with faux pink, blue, and white hydrangeas and pastel-color plastic eggs. Keep the arrangement informal, as if you plucked fistfuls of flowers to carry into the house. Tuck tufts of moss and sprigs of faux ivy and other greenery here and there, twirl greenery up and around the handle, and finish with pink and blue satin ribbons tied into a bow with trailing tails. Embellish the birds' nests with similar wisps of greenery and mini faux Robin eggs.

Favors: An Easter basket you make is so much more personal than a store-bought one. Buy small pastel-color baskets at a craft store or spray paint in a pastel shade. Buy pastel-colored Easter candy and cookies; bundle in clear or colored cellophane. Tie each bundle with ribbon, leaving a 2- or 3-inch cellophane tail peeking out. Line the basket with cellophane and arrange the bundles in it. Fill in with stuffed animals and lollipop bouquets.

Accent Pieces: Redefine the eggcup with these scalloped china teacups in spring colors. Use plastic or papier-mâché eggs if you are using them as decoration. Check craft, party, and home stores to find similar styles and patterns. Line birds' nests (available at craft stores) with moss, tuck in greenery, and nest them with small egg-shaped candies.

Flower-Covered Eggs: To make these eggs, start with Styrofoam® in any size of egg shapes. Working with a hot-glue gun, a section at a time, coat the eggs with glue and attach tiny silk flowers (available at craft stores). Hot-glue or pin a complementary-color tassel to the bottom of the egg and a loop of pastel ribbon to the top.

Upside-Down Apple Skillet Pie

- **1 stick butter**
- **½ cup packed brown sugar**
- **1 teaspoon cinnamon, *McCormick®***
- **1 can (21-ounce) apple pie filling, *Comstock®***
- **2 cups presliced apples, *Ready Pac® More Fruit***
- **1 Refrigerated piecrust, *Pillsbury®***
- **2 tablespoons apple juice concentrate, thawed, *Minute Maid®***
- **1 tablespoon granulated sugar**

1. Preheat oven to to 425 degrees F. In a 10-inch cast iron skillet or ovenproof pan, melt butter over medium-high heat. When butter has melted, stir in brown sugar and cinnamon. Cook until it begins to bubble. Stir in apple pie filling and apple slices.

2. Unroll piecrust and place over skillet. With a wooden spoon, push edges of piecrust into skillet. Brush with apple juice concentrate and sprinkle with sugar. Cut slit in top of crust to allow steam to escape.

3. Bake in preheated oven for 30 to 35 minutes or until crust is golden brown. Remove from oven and let cool 1 hour before slicing. Makes 6 servings.

Butter-Rum Coffee

- **1 shot butterscotch schnapps, *DeKuyper®***
- **1 shot vanilla rum, *Captain Morgan®***
- **½ shot Irish cream liqueur, *Baileys®***
- **Hot brewed coffee**
- **Frozen whipped topping, thawed, *Cool Whip®***

1. In a coffee mug, combine schnapps, rum, and Irish cream liqueur. Add coffee to fill mug. Top with whipped topping. Makes 1 drink.

Music: Judy Garland. Fred Astaire. Irving Berlin: The movie soundtrack from *Easter Parade* is a triple treat. And the mellow mood matches the table—light, festive, and utterly delicious.

Cream Cheese Sugar Cutouts

- **1 package (18-ounce) refrigerated sugar cookie dough, room temperature, *Pillsbury*®**
- **3 ounces cream cheese, softened, *Philadelphia*®**
- **¾ cup cake flour**
- **1 teaspoon vanilla extract, *McCormick*®**
- **Flour, for dusting work surface**
- **Colored sugars, frosting, and candies**

1. Preheat oven to 350 degrees F. Cut cookie dough into 8 pieces. In the bowl of an electric mixer, thoroughly combine dough pieces, cream cheese, flour, and vanilla. If dough is too soft, add additional flour as needed and place in refrigerator for 15 minutes.

2. On a lightly floured surface, roll dough out to ¼-inch thickness. Using your favorite cookie cutters, cut out cookies. Place on greased cookie sheets. Sprinkle with colored sugar.

3. Bake for 10 minutes or until edges are light golden brown. Cool completely on cooling rack. Decorate as desired with colored sugars, frosting, and candies. Makes about 24 cookies.

Food and Drink: Decorating Easter cookies with the kids is a fun family project, especially if you keep it simple. Cream Cheese Sugar Cutouts start with refrigerated slice-and-bake dough so you can spend more time on the fun stuff that makes your cookies special. Mix up a box of royal icing and thin it with water so it'll dry into a stiff, glossy glaze on your cookies. Divide the icing into bowls, tint it with a drop or two of food coloring to get the right pastel shades, then pour each shade into a plastic squirt bottle. This "squeeze" method allows you to do all kinds of fun effects and swirls—even write names—while keeping things neat. When it comes to toppings, the more the merrier, so set up a "sundae" bar of candies, sprinkles, and colored sugars—it's very orderly and the whole family can get involved. Remember to use toothpicks for creating decorative designs such as tie dye.

Valentine Chocolates

This sweet little buffet casts a subliminal spell on chocolate lovers—and that includes just about everyone. Eyes will be drawn right away to the bouquet of chocolates arranged in burnished gold urns. (Just line each with a glass or paper to make them food safe.) The palette is pure decadence, a blend of the vanilla creams, velvety caramels, intense dark chocolates, and milky cocoas found in a luxurious box of chocolates. And how can you go wrong setting it against the opulence of gold and crystal? The Renaissance feel of it all works beautifully as a Valentine to those you treasure most or segues gracefully into a setting for an after-theatre party, an anniversary event, or a New Year's Eve celebration that wishes everyone an abundance of riches in the year ahead. Guide guests to their seats with place card party favors: Wrap miniature boxes of chocolates in shimmering swaths of tulle tied with satiny ribbon and tuck a name card into each. The menu is sheer indulgence—mounds of Mocha Chip Scones coupled with Minty Chip Frappés—luscious against a woven tablecloth in subtle stripes of gold and cream. For a smooth finish, bring in the mochas and café au laits of the finest coffees, flavored with creamy liqueurs.

Centerpiece: A tiered gold-filigree candleholder drips crystals, adding jewel-like sparkle to the tablescape. Recreate the mood by dressing up any holder you have with inexpensive plastic crystals from the craft store. Surround the candles with edible luxury—cut-glass dishes filled with a chocolate-nut mix found at your favorite gourmet or candy shop.

Place Settings: A buffet makes life easy—just stack gold chargers and clear glass plates so guests can serve themselves.

Favors: Light gold napkins recall the buttery fillings in the richest of confections. The napkin rings are actually chunky woven bracelets—a take-home presentation made perfect.

Mocha Chip Scones

- 1/4 cup coffee, double strength, cooled
- 2 tablespoons heavy cream
- 1 large egg, lightly beaten
- 1 teaspoon vanilla extract, *McCormick®*
- 3 1/2 cups baking mix, *Bisquick®*
- 1/2 cup sugar
- 3/4 cup chopped special dark chocolate candy bars, *Hershey's®*
- 3/4 cup semisweet chocolate chips, *Nestlé®*
- 1 large egg, lightly beaten
- 1 tablespoon heavy cream
- White decorating sugar or sanding sugar
- Butter

1. Preheat oven to 350 degrees F.

2. In a small bowl, combine cooled double-strength coffee, cream, lightly beaten egg, and vanilla extract; set aside.

3. In a large mixing bowl, combine baking mix, sugar, special dark chocolate, and semisweet chocolate chips.

4. Add wet ingredients to dry ingredients and work into a crumbly dough. On a lightly floured surface, form dough into a 9-inch disk (approximately 1/2 inch thick). Cut into 12 wedges and place on ungreased cookie sheet; set aside.

5. In a small bowl, combine lightly beaten egg and 1 tablespoon cream. Brush tops of scones with egg mixture and sprinkle with decorating sugar.

6. Bake in preheated oven for 15 to 18 minutes or until golden brown. Serve warm with butter. Makes12 servings.

Minty Chip Frappé

- 2 scoops mint chocolate chip ice cream, *Breyers®*
- 1 cup crushed ice
- 1/2 cup evaporated milk, *Carnation®*
- 1/4 cup miniature chocolate pieces, *Nestlé®*
- 2 tablespoons chocolate-flavored syrup, *Hershey's®*

1. In blender, place ice cream, ice, evaporated milk, chocolate pieces, and chocolate-flavored syrup. Cover; turn blender to HIGH. Blend for about 2 minutes until mixture is smooth and frothy.

2. Pour into a large glass. Makes 1 drink.

New Year Dreams

Out with the old, in with the new! A white-on-white theme is classic yet simple, a dreamy way to toast the past and celebrate the future with family and friends. And while New Year's Eve is one of the year's most glamorous occasions, other events—like birthdays, weddings, and engagements—deserve special treatment too. Give the tabletop the allure of a dramatic ball gown with an elegant white tablecloth festooned on the sides. To shape, gather extra tablecloths or curtain panels into swags on each side and secure with a wide ribbon or strip of fabric pinned in place. Go for old-time Hollywood glamour with silver beads, ropes of crystal, and elegant candles nestled in glass and silver candleholders. (Use real crystal if you have it; if not, faux crystals give the same effect.) Crystal-Rum Cookies make a dressy dessert, stacked in etched-glass goblets that make their golden hue sparkle. Shimmer-tinis add another whisper of color, served in graceful glasses with a swan-neck stem. Their taste is well worth toasting—velvety vanilla vodka, pineapple, and Key lime juice, with a top note of cream of coconut, blended into a fitting concoction to bid the year a sweet farewell and ring in a new one so full of promise.

Place Settings: Glass plates stacked on faux silver chargers look luxurious. A white napkin gathered with a silver napkin ring embellished with a teardrop crystal ornament ups the opulence. **Centerpiece:** Silver-footed glass hurricanes lend an air of formality, filled with silver beads and a white taper candle. Flanked by crystal chandelier-style votive holders, they exude romance. **Accent Pieces:** A silver candy dish looks even more polished when silvered almonds rest inside. **Music:** Toast the night with *The Essential Tony Bennett* until it's time for "Auld Lang Syne."

Crystal-Rum Cookies

- 1 package (17.5-ounce) oatmeal cookie mix, ***Betty Crocker®***
- ⅓ cup canola oil, ***Wesson®***
- 1 large egg, lightly beaten
- 3 tablespoons dark rum, ***Myers's®***

1. Preheat oven to 375 degrees F.

2. In a large bowl, combine oatmeal cookie mix, canola oil, egg, and rum. Stir to form a dough. Drop by rounded tablespoons onto ungreased cookie sheet.

3. Bake in preheated oven for 9 to 11 minutes.* Remove from cookie sheet; cool on wire rack. Makes about 24 cookies.

***Note:** If you like, you can bake only as many cookies as you need. The cookie dough will keep, covered, in refrigerator for 4 to 5 days.

Shimmer-tini

- Ice cubes
- 2 shots vanilla vodka, ***Stoli®***
- 1 shot unsweetened pineapple juice, ***Dole®***
- ½ shot bottled Key lime juice, ***Nellie & Joe's®***
- 2 tablespoons cream of coconut, ***Coco Lopez®***

1. Fill a martini shaker with ice cubes. Add vodka, pineapple juice, Key lime juice, and cream of coconut. Shake vigorously. Strain into a martini glass. Makes 1 drink.

Place Card Favors: A bit of bubbly adds to the festivities. Write each guest's name on a self-adhesive label and stick it to the front of a split of champagne. Look for labels with a silver border or color a border on white labels with a metallic pen. A silver ribbon necktie dresses it up.

Colleen

Birthdays

Birthdays are a celebration of life, the first day of the next 365. Of the many milestones we honor—graduations, weddings, anniversaries—a birthdays is yours alone. Tradition holds them sacred; the candles on the cake, the "light of life." When we blow them out, it's said the smoke carries our wishes to heaven.

Of course, most of us wish that celebrating could be simpler—and it is with Semi-Homemade®! Dressing up a store-bought cake, mixing creative cocktails, making the main course deliciously easy, and sharing the secrets for setting a spectacular table is my birthday gift to you.

This chapter is filled with special ways to celebrate that special person, whoever it is. A Wisteria Wish grants your best friend or sister a queenly feast of Brie Quesadillas and Blueberry Sangria on a table of royal purples. Kids—or kids at heart—will eat up a Fountain Fantasy's candyland colors and sweet treats, a Fountain Angel Cake and Mocha Egg Creams (spiked or not—you choose). Gather the guys! Casino Night makes birthdays a big deal with cards, Cocojitos, and a round of Fruit Pizza, while A Harley Party picnic sizzles with Talk-of-the-Town New York Strips, Tangerine Teriyaki Ribs, and manly martinis against a biker backdrop of black and chrome.

Perhaps we love birthdays because they're a clean slate. Or maybe it's those Buttercream Cake Martinis that make it all seem so fun. Either way, Semi-Homemade® makes celebrating a piece of cake.

Creative Cakes

No food says "party!" quite like a cake, especially when it's someone's Big Day. Or maybe you're hosting a tea party, shower, or a just-because get-together with friends. Whatever the occasion, the first order of fun is to settle on a theme. Butterflies and blooms share the stage here, simply because I found their graceful designs on a slew of matching table accessories and fell in love with their flighty charm. You can find similar patterns by treasure hunting through craft and party stores for inspiring go-withs that capture the personality of your guest of honor. It's a pastel palette, with the primary pinks, purples, yellows and greens pulled from the buy-as-a-set plates. A butterfly-on-gingham tablecloth matches the window valance to pull it all together. What's to eat? Cakes, of course, and cocktails, too, starting with a Buttercream Cake Martini, a sweet lover's dream of butterscotch and cream. It's downright groovy how the Tie-Dyed Cupcakes give each guest a cake (or two) of their own while adding color with a clever spin art design. (Ready-made gel icings and a toothpick are all you need to pull it off.) Give the color wheel a final spin by sprinkling the sides of a white bakery cake with candy confetti and topping with a cupcake ornament.

Favors: This garden-theme butterfly box holds everything from recipe cards to keys. To make, mask the box's glass windows with paint tape and spray paint the wood trim a pale green. Remove tape. Cut the picket fence trim into four pieces, each cut to fit inside one window of the box. Squeeze hot glue onto the front of the picket panels, position them against the glass, and press into place. Hot-glue three silk butterflies to the top.

Window Treatment: A coordinating cornice board gives a cozy cocoon feeling. Cover a piece of plywood with fabric matching your table; mount to window. Gather the fabric into pleats and staple into place. Attach silk butterflies.

Laura

Centerpiece: A graceful sage green vase filled with Stargazer lilies plays off the butterflies. The petal's shape looks just like butterfly wings. Mini high-heel ceramic shoes with butterfly buckles are brilliant vessels for votive candles; placed on either side of the centerpiece, they add yet another note of whimsy.

Place Settings: A quartet of butterfly-shape plates is the starting point for the table's flight of fancy. With plates this pretty, let them stand solo to show them off. Oversize napkins in the softest sage tuck under the plates. They're meant to stay on the table throughout dinner; simply place them on the diagonal and the opposite points will puddle right into the guests' laps.

Place Cards: Store-bought butterfly holders are ready for place cards. Buy plain white cards and add colorful butterfly stickers or rubber stamps. Vary the colors used for each guest's name to echo the table's multicolor palette.

Accent Pieces: Add height and charm to the tablescape with towering cocktail glasses, soaring lily bouquets, and a decorative rack stacked with butterfly-handled teacups. Silk butterflies hover above the cup rack, held in place with a bit of glue. It's the little details that make this table so special—the glasses' tall, wavy stems, the ruffled saucers, and the way the dots in the silverware handles echo the speckles in the butterfly wings and flower petals.

Tie-Dyed Cupcakes

1 box (18.25-ounce) white cake mix, *Betty Crocker®*
1¼ cups white grape juice, *Ocean Spray®*
⅓ cup canola oil, *Wesson®*
1 bottle (1.25-ounce) colored snowflake sprinkles, *Cake Mate®*
1 bottle (1.85-ounce) rainbow sprinkles, *Cake Mate®*
1 can (12-ounce) ready-to-spread whipped fluffy white frosting, *Betty Crocker®*
Assorted colors decorating gels, *Cake Mate®*

1. Preheat oven to 350 degrees F. Line twenty-four 2½-inch muffin cups with cupcake papers; set aside.

2. In a large bowl, place cake mix, grape juice, and canola oil. Using a handheld electric mixer, beat on medium speed for 1 minute. Scrape sides of bowl; add both bottles of sprinkles. Beat 30 seconds more. Using a ladle, fill each lined muffin cup ⅔ full.

3. Bake in preheated oven for 21 to 26 minutes or until a toothpick inserted into center of cupcake comes out clean.

4. Remove from oven. Place muffin pans on wire racks; let stand about 30 minutes or until completely cool.

5. Spread 2 tablespoons frosting on each cupcake. Using assorted colors of decorating gels, start in the middle of each cupcake and make circles outward to the edge. Using a toothpick, begin at the edge of the cupcake and drag the tip of toothpick to the center of the cupcake to make a spiderweb effect. Repeat this step around each cupcake, turning the cupcake as you go. Makes 24 cupcakes.

Buttercreme Cake Martini

1 shot spiced rum, *Captain Morgan®*
½ shot butterscotch schnapps, *DeKuyper®*
½ shot vanilla schnapps, *DeKuyper®*
1 shot half-and-half
Ice cubes
Candy confetti, for garnish

1. Add all ingredients, except candy confetti, to cocktail shaker filled with ice. Shake well and strain into a martini glass. Garnish with a sprinkle of candy confetti. Makes 1 drink.

On Lily Pond

Invite a few frogs over and raise everyone's spirits. Partygoers will get a kick out of stealing away to your own private lily pond, whatever the big event. Maybe the guest of honor is bounding ahead to another year, jumping up a rung on the career ladder, or leaping into a brand new pad. Or maybe you just saw all these cute frogs in the craft store and thought life could use a little lightening up. Either way, play with a palette of greens for this tablescape, starting with a frolicking frog centerpiece made of a durable resin you'll use again and again. Fill in with freshwater accents in hues ranging from moss to avocado to lichen—all present in the plaid fabric table covering—then add bunches of yellow and white lilies to bring even more prettiness to your pond. Munch on a splashy tray of precut crudités and quick Fried Chicken Salad that lets you spring from kitchen to table in no time at all. The Porch Swing Iced Tea will keep the party hopping right along with a shot of citrus vodka and a sprig of mint. For a fitting finale, try Lemon Cream Squares—a zippy mix of lemon and lime, garnished with a raspberry or mint leaf.

Place Cards: A frog resting on a lily pad place card—how apropros! Cut brown paper in circles to mimic lily pads and attach to faux lily flowers snipped off at the stem. Use clear fishing line to attach a fishing bob to a ceramic frog ornament, then pose the frog on one of the flower petals.

Fashion: A simple scoop-neck green cotton t-shirt dress looks lily fresh.

Place Settings: Woven white circular place mats pick up on the lily pad theme, while raw linen-look napkins are outdoorsy in a soft sage. Cast your net for coordinating dishes, like these shiny river green plates, topped with smaller accent plates sporting a lily design.

Accent Pieces: What's a pond without some moss? Moss-covered fencing or chicken wire rolled lengthwise down the table makes a trellislike table runner. (Buy it in rolls at craft stores.) Faux leafy tree topiaries in white lattice pots flank the frog centerpiece, while a ribbed green ceramic tea set is both fashionable and functional.

Music: Try the cast recording of *A Year with Frog and Toad*. For a whimsical note, play the *Muppet Movie* soundtrack, featuring—who else!—Kermit the Frog.

Lemon Cream Squares

- **1 box (18.25-ounce) lemon cake mix, *Betty Crocker*®**
- **1 stick butter, softened**
- **1 egg**
- **2 packages (8 ounces each) cream cheese, softened, *Philadelphia*®**
- **1/3 cup sugar**
- **1 box (3-ounce) lime gelatin, *Jell-O*®**
- **2 eggs**
- **Raspberries and/or mint leaves, for garnish**

1. Preheat oven to 350 degrees F. Lightly spray 9×13-inch baking pan with cooking spray; set aside.

2. In a large mixing bowl, combine cake mix, butter, and egg. Beat with an electric mixer on low speed until combined. Press cake mixture evenly into prepared pan; set aside.

3. In a medium mixing bowl, beat cream cheese, sugar, and lime gelatin on medium speed until creamy. Add eggs and beat until smooth. Spread cream cheese mixture over cake layer.

4. Bake for 40 to 45 minutes or until bars just begin to pull away from edges of pan. Cool completely before cutting into squares. Garnish with raspberries or mint leaves. Makes 15 squares.

Fried Chicken Salad

- 1 box (12-ounce) popcorn chicken, *Tyson*®
- ½ cup ranch dressing, *Hidden Valley*®
- 2 teaspoons BBQ seasoning, *McCormick® Grill Mates*®
- 8 cups romaine or iceburg lettuce, chopped
- 1 cucumber, thinly sliced (optional)

1. Preheat oven to 425 degrees F. Line baking sheet with aluminum foil. Place popcorn chicken on baking sheet. Bake for 8 to10 minutes or until crispy and heated through.

2. Mix together ranch dressing and seasoning in small bowl; set aside.

3. Divide lettuce onto 4 cold plates. Top with chicken pieces and, if desired, cucumber slices. Drizzle dressing over salad. Makes 4 servings.

Porch Swing Iced Tea

- Ice cubes
- 1 shot citrus vodka, *Skyy*®
- Iced tea
- Fresh mint sprigs

1. Fill highball glass with ice cubes. Pour in vodka and your favorite iced tea.

2. Garnish with mint and serve. Makes 1 drink.

A Wisteria Wish

Ah, wisteria...Its soothing shades and feathery blooms have charmed gardeners for centuries. When the party moves from outside to inside, recreate that alfresco feel flawlessly. Have the ladies for high tea, host a bridal shower, or honor your parents' anniversary. Freshening wisteria's royal purples and soft lavenders with green and white accents is stunningly elegant, without a hint of stuffiness. Ground the table with a purple plaid cloth and lavender runner that bring out the flowers' softer side, layering in darker shades in the place setting, centerpiece, and above. For place settings, a clear glass plate tops pale green plates painted with purple wisteria to make a setting worthy of your grandmother's best silver. Create accent pieces with the look of wisteria luxuriating across a pergola by hanging faux wisteria branches to the ceiling above the table or to the light fixture. The menu is divinely easy. Both appetizer and dessert—Brie Quesadillas and Apricot Shortcakes—are served on easy-to-make pedestals—flip two pale green wisteria-painted urns upside down and top with matching plates. For a final flourish, bring out the drink of the day—Blueberry Sangria—in stemmed hurricanes showcasing its lovely layers.

Centerpiece: Willowy wisteria is shown to best effect in a tall vase. A painted-on wisteria design matches the dishes and food pedestals and echoes the flowers inside. The vase's gentle curves mirror the curvaceous cocktail glasses; the colors are equally compatible, pulling the tablescape's elements together. **Place Card Favors:** To make the dainty trinket box place card, cover a small cardboard craft box or photo frame with a pretty purple fabric coordinating with the table linens. Cut a circle of purple paper to fit inside a scrapbooking medallion and write the guest's name in the center. The lace-collar effect adds another grace note, as does varying the fabrics and medallion shapes. **Music:** Play up the Southern charm with *Some Hearts* by Carrie Underwood.

Blueberry Sangria

1½ cups frozen blueberries, *Dole®*
1 can (12-ounce) pink lemonade frozen concentrate, *Minute Maid®*
1 bottle (750 ml) Chardonnay
3 cups lemon-lime soda, *Sprite®*
½ cup cognac, *Hennessy®*
Ice cubes

1. In a large pitcher, combine all ingredients and stir well. Refrigerate for 1 hour to blend flavors. Pour in glasses over ice. Makes 8 drinks.

Brie Quesdillas

8 flour tortillas, taco size, *Mission®*
5 ounces Brie cheese, sliced
3 ounces prosciutto, thinly sliced
4 figs, sliced
1 cup shredded Monterey Jack cheese, *Kraft®*
2 tablespoons vegetable oil
½ cup fig preserves, *Braswell's®*

1. Lay out 4 tortillas; top each tortilla with half of the brie. Divide prosciutto and figs and place on top of Brie. Top with Jack cheese and remaining tortillas.

2. In a skillet large enough to fit tortillas, heat vegetable oil over medium heat. When oil is hot, carefully fry both sides of quesadillas for 2 to 3 minutes or until golden brown, turning with a spatula. Serve with fig preserves. Makes 4 servings.

Apricot Shortcakes

1 package (8-ounce) mascarpone cheese, *BelGioioso®*
1 container (8-ounce) frozen extra-creamy whipped topping, thawed, *Cool Whip®*
1 teaspoon shredded lemon zest
½ teaspoon almond extract, *McCormick®*
Pinch salt
1 package (5-ounce) individual dessert sponge cakes, *Van de Kamp's®
1 can (15-ounce) apricot halves in heavy syrup, *Del Monte®*
2 tablespoons brandy, *Christian Brothers®*
Slivered almonds, toasted, (optional)

1. In a large bowl, whisk mascarpone cheese to soften. Stir in half of the container of whipped topping, lemon zest, almond extract, and salt. Fill each sponge cake with some of the cheese mixture.

2. Drain apricots, reserving syrup. Set apricots aside. In a small saucepan, over high heat, combine the reserved apricot syrup and brandy; cook until thick. Add apricots.

3. Spoon apricot mixture over sponge cakes. Top with remaining whipped topping. If desired, garnish with almonds. Makes 6 servings.

*__Note:__ If sponge cakes are not available, use sliced pound cake.

Lemon Tree

Old-timey lemonade is usually considered a casual beverage—something we sip on the porch when the weather is warm and the chores are done. For this party, I've elevated lemonade—and lemons—from simple to sophisticated and made them the center of a celebration honoring a spring birthday. Parlay this party into anything you want, as long as the occasion is genteel. Try a lemony twist on a tea party, a lawn party, or even a dressy hat party taking you back to a more serene era. The mood is the same—light, airy, and feminine. Citrus hues dominate the tablescape and the food, with a yellow and white small-print runner layered over a yellow floral weave tablecloth to make a sunny backdrop for crisp white accents and glossy greenery. For party favors, cloches for each guest include lemon-scented items tucked inside on a white plate. Three-inch-wide voile bows on the top of each lend a dainty touch. The menu is a delicious contrast—much like lemons themselves—sweet yet tart, creamy yet refreshingly elegant. Fresh blueberries add color to Lemon Pudding Brûleé, while Lemon Cream Martinis are worth the splurge. Served in martini glasses with crushed lemon drops garnishing the rim, they tell your guests, "I'm glad you came."

Centerpiece: Choose pale yellow lemonade served in a tall, curvy glass canister with an etched design that underscores the party's femininity. Lemonade is the defining accessory, with fresh lemon slices as pretty garnishes. **Place Settings:** Keep to the theme with citrus-hued china on a yellow and white patterned runner, accessorized with your best silverware. **Accent Pieces:** Purchased miniature lemon topiaries in white lattice pots flank the centerpiece, adding height. Make them by hot-glueing or wiring whole lemons to any green topiary. **Place Cards:** To make these that double as napkin rings, use a cookie cutter to trace and cut a daisy shape out of white card stock. Draw a yellow border around the edge, write your guest's name, and punch two holes below the name. Wrap a thin yellow ribbon around a rolled napkin and place the place card on top. Thread the ends of the ribbon through the holes in the place card and tie into a bow.

Lemon Pudding Brûlée

- 1 box (3.4-ounce) instant lemon pudding mix, *Jell-O®*
- 2 cups cold milk
- ½ pint fresh blueberries
- ¼ cup sugar (optional)
- Frozen whipped topping, thawed, *Cool Whip®*

1. Preheat broiler. Place pudding mix in a medium bowl. Add cold milk; whisk for 2 minutes. Chill in the refrigerator for 5 minutes.

2. Count out 12 blueberries; set aside for garnish. Fold remaining berries into the pudding. Divide pudding into four 8-ounce broiler-proof casseroles. Refrigerate until ready to serve.

3. If desired, sprinkle 1 tablespoon of the sugar on each of the casseroles. Place casseroles on a baking sheet. Broil 6 inches from heat for 2 to 3 minutes or until sugar has caramelized, rotating the baking sheet so the sugar caramelizes evenly.

4. Garnish with reserved berries. Top with whipped topping. Makes 4 servings.

Lemon Cream Martini

- Ice cubes
- 2 shots vanilla vodka, *Stoli®*
- ½ shot lemon liqueur, *Limoncello®*
- Lemon-flavor glass rimmer, *Stirrings®*
- Splash lemon-lime soda, *Sprite®*
- Fresh blueberries (optional)

1. Fill a martini shaker with ice cubes. Add vodka and lemon liqueur. Wet rim of martini glass and coat with lemon-flavored rimmer. Shake vodka mixture vigorously. Strain into prepared martini glass. Add carbonated beverage. If desired, garnish with blueberries. Makes 1 drink.

Fountain Fantasy

As a child, I had a favorite book about a little girl who was accidentally locked inside a soda fountain all night. I'd read over and over about the endless lollipops, cupcakes, and milkshakes that she ate. I'm grown up now, but I'm still a sucker for soda fountains, so I decided to recreate the fantasy with a goodie night of my own. Give kids or adults the best birthday ever or think Movie Night or Girls' Night In. With a theme of candy, candy, candy, dessert lovers will find this party a dream come true. It's a dream for the hostess, too, with an easy-to-make tablescape that mixes real candies with candy crafts. Start with a medley of ribbon stripes and spirited pastels that pop against a mint green tablecloth. Go for a menu that's pure nostalgia food given a grown-up twist—Bleu Cheese-Bacon Burgers, spicy French fries, and candy à la carte. Chill out with old-fashioned fountain drinks like Spiked Mocha Egg Creams, served in ruffled sundae glasses. Throw on a CD by Sammy Davis Jr., the ultimate candy man, or the *Charlie and the Chocolate Factory* soundtrack. Top it off with a tower of treats that puts everyone on cloud nine.

Favors: A cupcake-topped recipe box makes a take-home treat, filled with the party recipes printed on pastel cards. Cover the box in mint and white fabric to match the table, then finish by hot-gluing tiny craft cupcakes to the lid for decoration, to the front for the knobs, and upside down to the bottom for feet.

Place Cards: A jar of candy makes an edible place card. Spray paint the lid green. Write your guest's name on a piece of colored construction paper, insert it in a cardholder from a party store, and anchor with a mini clothespin in a contrasting color. Hot-glue to the lid of a see-through container filled with pastel candies.

Centerpiece: Dessert stars as the center of attention. Choose candy-striped ceramic or plastic containers in assorted shapes. Stack them pyramid style on a matching cake stand and secure with hot glue. Fill with candies. Stick large swirl and spiral lollipops into containers. **Accent Pieces:** Capture all the colors of the table—blues, pinks, yellows, and greens—by filling glass boxes with gumdrops, mints, or colored almonds; hot-glue dessert ornaments on the lids and guests can dig right in.

Fountain Angel Cake

Cake

1 store-bought angel food cake or pound cake ring
1 jar (10-ounce) lemon curd, *Dickinson's*®
2 cups frozen whipped topping, thawed, divided, *Cool Whip*®

Icing

3 cups powdered sugar
½ cup lemonade, frozen concentrate, thawed, *Minute Maid*®
1 tablespoon lemon gelatin, *Jell-O*®
¼ cup frozen whipped topping, thawed, *Cool Whip*®

1. For the cake, with a serrated knife, level the bigger end of the cake. This will be the bottom. Slice off top inch of cake. Carefully set aside—do not break. Scoop out a trench in the cake for the filling.*Set aside.

2. In a bowl, combine lemon curd and 1 cup whipped topping. Stir to combine. Carefully fold in remaining 1 cup of whipped topping until just combined. Do not overstir. Fill center of cake with filling and return the top of the cake into place.

3. For the icing, in a large bowl, combine icing ingredients. Stir until thoroughly combined, making sure that all lumps are dissolved. Drizzle icing over cake and serve. Makes 10 servings.
***Tip:** Removed portion of cake can be frozen and used for a trifle at a later time. Set aside.

Spiked Mocha Egg Cream

2 tablespoons chocolate syrup, *Hershey's*®
1 shot coffee liqueur, *Starbucks*®
¾ cup milk, cold
¾ cup seltzer water, cold

1. In a 12-ounce glass, stir together chocolate syrup, coffee liqueur, and milk. Top with seltzer water and stir.

2. Serve immediately. Makes 1 drink.

Place Settings: Pastel-striped plates coordinate with pink and purple napkins, playing off the colorful centerpiece to dazzling effect. Serve the fries in containers matching the centerpiece for help-yourself symmetry. They're a treat all ages will enjoy.

Bleu Cheese-Bacon Burgers

Bleu Cheese Butter
4 tablespoons butter
2 tablespoons bleu cheese crumbles, *Treasure Cave*®
4 slices bacon, cut into ½-inch pieces and crisp-cooked
Burgers
1½ pounds lean ground beef
½ cup bleu cheese crumbles, *Treasure Cave*®
¼ cup real bacon pieces, *Hormel*®
1 tablespoon Montreal steak seasoning, *McCormick® Grill Mates*®
Salt and black pepper to taste
Onion rolls
Lettuce, tomato, onion
Sliced avocado, optional

1. For the butter, in a small bowl with a fork, smash together butter and 2 tablespoons bleu cheese crumbles; set aside.

2. For the burgers, in a mixing bowl, stir to combine ground beef, ⅓ cup bleu cheese crumbles, bacon pieces, and steak seasoning. Wet your hands to prevent sticking and shape into 4 patties slightly larger than the buns. Cover with plastic and set aside in refrigerator.

3. Preheat broiler. Place burgers on wire rack over foil-lined baking sheet or broiler pan. Broil 6 inches from heat source for 4 to 5 minutes per side for medium.

4. Serve hot on toasted onion roll spread with bleu cheese butter, lettuce, tomato, onion, and, if desired, sliced avocado. Makes 4 servings.

Chili Fountain Fries

1 bag (28-ounce) frozen steak fries, thawed, *Ore-Ida*®
2 tablespoons canola oil, *Wesson*®
1 tablespoon chili seasoning, *McCormick*®
Barbecue sauce, for dipping, *Heinz*®

1. Preheat broiler. Place frozen fries on a foil-lined baking sheet.

2. Toss fries with oil and chili seasoning.

3. Broil fries for 8 to 12 minutes, turning once or until desired degree of crispness. Serve hot with your favorite barbecue sauce for dipping. Makes 4 servings.

Kim

Casino Night

Let the good times roll! Who needs a trip to Vegas when you can set up a mini casino right in your own living room? Whatever the occasion—a birthday, an anniversary, or just hey, why not?—a casino-theme tablescape is sure to be a hands-on favorite with your guests. The palette is reds, blacks, and greens, with a game table serving as the food table too. If you don't have a game table, improvise by covering any table with green felt. No need to hem—no sewing makes it easy. Just buy it at the fabric store and cut to fit. The decor is simple—plenty of poker chips, cards, and dice, plus a tabletop roulette wheel that invites guests to spin and win. Whether you're playing for prizes, favors, or just for fun, keep drinks and food flowing in playing card plates and poker-theme bowls that double as décor. Chips and dips are a natural, but a Chicken Caesar Pizza Salad feeds a full house, while dessert—a colorful fruit pizza—doubles as a centerpiece on a pedestal bowl. Coconut rum, lime juice, and a fresh mint garnish turn a mojito into a Cocojito that's better than a royal flush. The decorations are reusable, so store them and make Casino Night at your place a monthly event. After all, the whole table goes home a winner.

Favors: Take-home favors are sure to be a deal for your guests. Purchase unfinished wooden recipe boxes from your local craft store. Paint the base of the box black and the lid red. Hot-glue playing cards around the base, leaving a stripe of black showing at the bottom. Finish with a few plastic dice hot-glued to the top and fill with the party recipes, playing cards, poker chips, or even candies—red and black candies would be perfect. When you're making boxes by the bunch, set up a craft table and put them together assembly-line style, and it'll go faster. **Fashion:** Black? You bet! It's the color of the evening, and my peek-a-boo wrap sweater makes style a done deal.

Kim
Sandra
BICYCLE

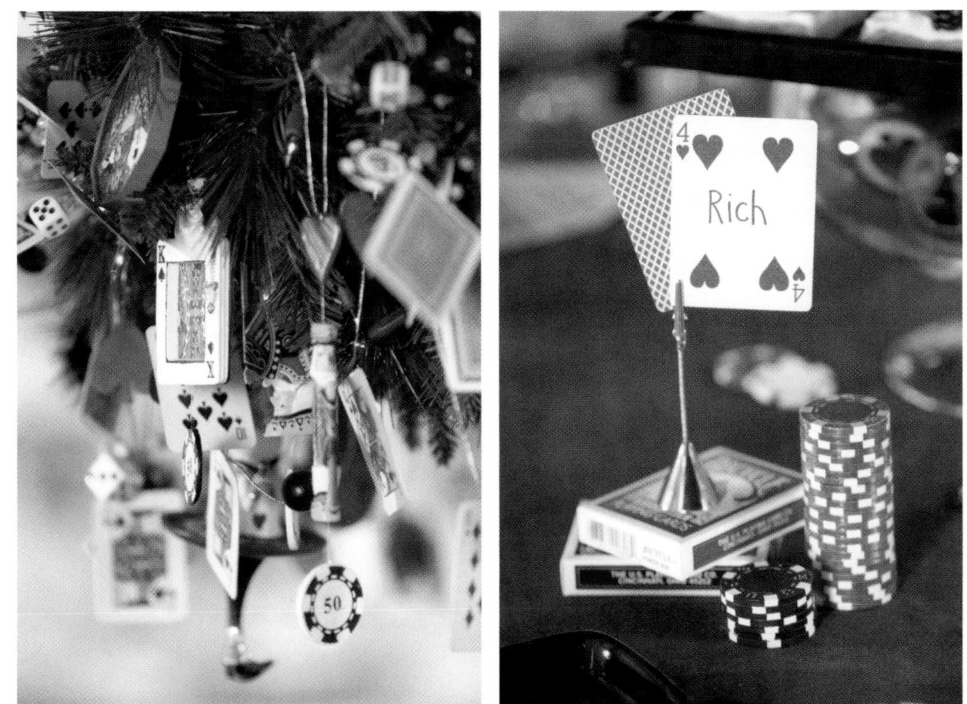

Cocojito

- 2 **shots coconut rum, *Bacardi*®**
- 5 **fresh mint leaves, torn**
- ½ **shot cream of coconut, *Coco Lopez*®**
- **Splash lime juice, *Rose's*®**
- **Club soda, *Schweppes*®**
- **Ice Cubes**
- **Mint sprigs, for garnish**

1. Add the first 4 ingredients to a cocktail shaker filled with ice cubes.

2. Shake several times and pour into chilled highball glass. Top with club soda and garnish with a sprig of mint. Makes 1 drink.

Centerpiece: When it comes to the centerpiece, it's dealer's choice. A bowl filled with playing card ornaments and topped with a glass platter of Fruit Pizza makes a help-yourself centerpiece for the table. For a more elaborate arrangement, turn a large card-motif serving bowl upside down, set a smaller bowl on top and hot glue a black plate on that. Scatter chips and stack red and black snack bowls, jumbo foam dice and playing cards up, down, and all around for a go-anywhere focal piece.

Place Settings: Fun poker plates come in groups of four—diamonds, hearts, spades, and clubs. Finger foods and paper napkins in red and black keep it simple and make cleanup quick. (If you need utensils, purchase black or red plastic.)

Accent Pieces: A little mood lighting is what the table needs. To make a poker party chandelier, start with lit holiday greenery. Attach a faux lit wreath or sprigs of greenery to your overhead light fixture. Hole-punch the top of several dozen playing cards and swag them around the greenery with gold or red cord. Follow with card-theme ornaments hung from the greenery with long ornament hooks. Hang dice, poker chips, beads, or cardboard cutouts of the card suits to finish.

Place Cards: Hold-'em, don't fold-'em with personalized playing cards that invite guests to take a seat. To make, write each guest's name on a playing card and tuck it in a silver clip cardholder perched atop stacked decks of playing cards.

Music: Play jazzy music, such as *The Dirty Boogie* by The Brian Setzer Orchestra.

Fruit Pizza

- canola oil cooking spray, Mazola® Pure®
- 1 stick butter, softened
- 1 package (8-ounce) cream cheese, softened, *Philadelphia®*
- ¾ cup powdered sugar
- 1 teaspoon almond extract, *McCormick®*
- 1 can (13.8-ounce) refrigerated pizza crust dough, *Pillsbury®*
- 1 tablespoon honey, *SueBee®*
- 1 tablespoon water
- 1 bag (12-ounce) frozen peach slices, thawed, *Dole®*
- 1 bag (12-ounce) frozen strawberrie slices, thawed, *Dole®*
- 1 bag (12-ounce) frozen mixed berries, thawed, *Dole®*

1. Preheat oven to 425 degrees F. Lightly spray a baking sheet with cooking spray; set aside.

2. In a mixing bowl, combine softened butter, cream cheese, sugar, and almond extract; beat with hand mixer on low speed until smooth and creamy. Set aside.

3. Combine honey and water in a small bowl. Stir until honey is dissolved. Set aside.

4. Unroll pizza dough and place on prepared baking sheet. Press dough out firmly with fingers to form a 13x9-inch rectangle. Brush with honey mixture and bake in preheated oven for 8 to 10 minutes or until crust is golden brown.

5. Remove crust from oven. Let cool. Spread with cream cheese mixture and arrange fruit on top. Makes 8 servings.

Chicken Caesar Pizza Salad

- ¾ pound chicken tenders, *Tyson®*
- ½ cup Caesar salad dressing, plus 2 tablespoons, *WishBone®*
- 1 12-inch thin pizza crust, *Boboli®*
- 1¾ cups shredded mozzarella and Asiago cheese, *Sargento®*
- ¼ cup shredded Parmesan cheese, *Kraft®*
- 4 cups hearts of romaine, shredded, *Ready Pac®*
- 1 tablespoon lemon juice, *ReaLemon®*
- ¼ cup Caesar salad dressing, *WishBone®*
- ¼ cup shredded Parmesan cheese, *Kraft®*
- 1 cup seasoned croutons, *Marie Callender's®*

1. Set up grill for direct cooking over medium heat. Oil grate when ready to start cooking.

2. In a bowl, combine chicken tenders with ½ cup salad dressing; set aside. Brush pizza crust with remaining 2 tablespoons of dressing and top with cheese blend and ¼ cup Parmesan; set aside.

3. Remove chicken from marinade and cook on hot oiled grill for 3 to 4 minutes per side or until just done. Remove from grill and place on top of pizza.

4. Slide pizza onto grill and cook, covered, 8 to 10 minutes or until cheese has melted and begun to bubble.

5. While pizza is cooking, toss shredded romaine with lemon juice. Add ¼ cup dressing and ¼ cup Parmesan. Toss and set aside.

6. Remove pizza from grill and cut into wedges. Top with salad and garnish with croutons. Serve immediately. Makes 4 servings.

Kim
PLAYING CARDS
1 TO 6
19 TO 24

HEDDEN
MCM
sparco

Race Car Daze

A day at the races is a blast for everyone—men, women, and kids—so start your engines and let the fun begin! The setting moves right to your backyard to help you host a special guy's birthday party, a race day brunch, or the ultimate power lunch. Race car reds are the main attraction, with whites and chromes to make things sparkle. The table is a classic, clothed in red-and-white picnic checks, swagged on the sides, and pinched in the middle to call attention to the tall cake centerpiece. The tablescape has more curves than a racetrack with oilcan flower vases, hubcap chargers, and assorted car parts transformed into creative party decor. (Buy it all new to keep things shiny.) The food's speedy to prepare—and it'll go just as fast! A step above picnic fare, it starts with Pineapple-Seafood Gumbo, a double treat served inside a scooped-out pineapple. Bleu-Stuffed Steak is stick-to-your-ribs guy food, dressed up with a creamy wine-cheese stuffing. That four-layer cake is waiting at the finish line for those with room for dessert.

Accent Pieces: Red and white flowers—peonies, tulips, roses—tag team the centerpiece cake. The twist? They're arranged in new silver oilcans, positioned in a lug nut wrench. You'll need four cans of flowers for each grouping. **Place Settings:** Red and white racing stripes rim stacked plates set on hubcap chargers. Top with rolled-up tea towel napkins in red and white, cinched with a hose clamp. **Place Cards:** Make place cards by printing guests' names on white self-stick labels on red cards. Mount on shiny new spark plugs.

Centerpiece: A grand four-layer cake claims the winner's circle, sitting proudly on a wheelbase pedestal. It's ready in no time when you start with a pair of two-layer store-bought cakes, stacked and iced into one with swirls of canned frosting that is flavored with your favorite extact (try rum). Decorate the top with a circle of Red Hots® with crossed racing flags waving victoriously in the center. Set the cake on a clear glass platter and balance that on a round clear acrylic tray set inside the wheelbase.

Favors: Guests won't go home empty-handed. Clip silver tire gauges onto red-and-chrome thermal cups for a color-cued takeaway. A red box of Comfort Foods® popcorn (go to http://www.helpusa.org/comfortfoods) makes it a two-for-one. And is the birthday boy in for a treat! A red toolbox makes a nifty beverage bar—good for food service too—but once the party's over, he can take it home as a gift.

Food and Drink: These racy red cocktails go down fast. Serve in long, tall glasses that play up their color, accented with silvery sparklers attached to the straws. Red wine makes an easy punch alternative that pairs well with the hearty steak.

Fashion: I'm suited up and race-car ready, but you can show your colors in casual red and white sweats or a racing jacket and jeans.

Music: Energetic music, like *Wild Child* by Lou Reed, is just the speed for a day at the track. Or give the *Days of Thunder* soundtrack a spin around the CD.

Pineapple-Seafood Gumbo

- **3 pineapples, halved and scooped**
- **1 cup pineapple, chopped**
- **1 can (13.5-ounce) lite coconut milk, *Taste of Thai®***
- **½ cup fresh cilantro, chopped**
- **2 teaspoons Thai seasoning, *Spice Islands®***
- **½ pound bay scallops, cleaned**
- **½ pound rock shrimp, cleaned**
- **1 pound cod, cut into 1-inch pieces**
- **Fresh cilantro, for garnish**

1. Set up grill for direct cooking over medium heat. Oil grate when ready to start cooking.

2. Cut pineapples in half and scoop out flesh to create bowl. Reserve 1 cup of finely chopped pineapple. Wrap bottoms of 6 pineapple halves with double layer of heavy-duty foil.

3. In a medium bowl, combine reserved pineapple, coconut milk, cilantro, and Thai seasoning. Fill each pineapple bowl halfway full of broth mixture.

4. Place pineapple bowls on hot oiled grill. Cover grill and cook until broth begins to simmer (approximately 15 to 20 minutes).

5. Once simmering, divide seafood among bowls. Close grill and cook for 5 minutes or until fish is opaque and flakes easily with a fork.

6. Remove seafood bowls from grill. Carefully remove foil and serve garnished with fresh cilantro. Makes 6 servings.

Indoor method: Preheat oven to 400 degrees F. Prepare pineapple bowls and fill as directed. Place bowls on foil-lined sheet pan and roast in preheated oven until broth begins to simmer, about 25 to 30 minutes. Add seafood to bowls and continue roasting until seafood is cooked through, about 5 to 10 minutes. Remove from oven and serve as directed.

Bleu-Stuffed Steak

- **4 beef tenderloin filets**
- **2 cups dry red wine**
- **2 tablespoons garlic and herb dressing mix, *Good Seasons®***
- **2 teaspoons ground black pepper**
- **1 jar marinated mushrooms, finely chopped, *California Girl®***
- **¼ cup bleu cheese crumbles, *Treasure Cave®***
- **1 teaspoon Italian seasoning, *Good Seasons®***

1. Rinse steaks and pat dry. Place in zip-top plastic bag and add red wine, dressing mix, and pepper. Squeeze air out of bag and seal. Marinate in refrigerator for 1 to 3 hours.

2. Set up grill for direct cooking over high heat. Oil grate when ready to start cooking.

3. In a bowl, combine chopped mushrooms, bleu cheese, and Italian seasoning; set aside.

4. Remove steaks from marinade and discard marinade. Cut a pocket into the side of each steak, being careful not to cut through. Stuff steaks with mushroom mixture and secure with toothpick. Place on hot oiled grill and cook for 5 to 7 minutes per side for medium doneness. Remove from grill. Remove toothpicks and serve hot. Makes 4 servings.

Indoor method: Preheat oven to 400 degees F. Follow directions for preparing steaks. Heat 2 tablespoons oil in ovenproof skillet over medium-high heat. Sear steaks on both sides until browned, 3 to 4 minutes. Place skillet in preheated oven for 12 to 16 minutes for medium doneness.

HARLEY-DAVIDSON

A Harley® Party

There's something about a Harley®. Maybe it's the sound of the engine purring to life—or the feel of the wind whipping past as you fly forward on winged wheels—or the freedom of owning the open road. Even if you aren't a rider, you can enjoy the ambience, so the next time a birthday rolls around, get ready for a road trip out to the patio. A biker theme gives a party a sense of adventure, especially if a sleek motorcycle is the guest of honor. If you don't have one, borrow one for fast ambience, or call a local dealer to see if you can rent one for the day. Build off that main piece with a bold black and white tablescape that starts with a silvery nubbed silk tablecloth and finishes with fun black and white tableware. Think macho for the menu. Hot-off-the-grill steaks and cool martinis make a powerful pair, with zesty Tangerine Teriyaki Ribs, deli sides, and crusty store-bought bread rounding out the menu. A silver pedestal of white cupcakes bearing black candles is a delicious sweet end to a night of freewheeling fun.

Place Settings: The black, white, and chrome place setting takes its cue from the colors of everybody's favorite "bad boy" toy. Get the table gleaming with glass and silver, then finish out the place setting with stacked square chargers and ornate round plates, topped with black napkins tucked in polka dot bowls. The Swirls and polka dots are surprisingly compatible and playful, showing how different shapes and patterns can harmonize beautifully. Black-handled silverware and black-stemmed wine glasses add eye-catching detail.

Accent Pieces: Let the gaming begin! Think games of chance, with tic-tac-toe boards, dice, poker chips, playing cards, chess pieces, and checkers as functional decor. A black photo frame hosts a printout of the menu, while self-serve snacks and beverages let guests help themselves. Bowls of black olives on white cocktail picks, sleek chrome and black cocktail shakers, black martini glasses with swanlike stems, even the black and white vodka bottle, all take on the party palette. An eclectic collection of black chairs illustrates how color can link a variety of styles.

Music: Biker boogies are a must. Spin *20th Century Masters—The Millennium Collection: The Best of .38 Special.*

Fashion: Comfy jeans and black boots, glammed up with a beaded black shirt, are biker chic. Don't forget that helmet and your trusty shades!

Centerpiece: The center of the table is pure glass. Mix shapely glass candelabra with statuesque candlesticks, all bearing black taper candles, to add height and glamour to the table. When darkness hits, the shimmer of the candlelight off the glass and silver is mesmerizing.

Napkins: To add a little more glitz to the tablescape, enclose black napkins in jazzy napkin rings that can go home with guests. Buy one rope of shiny black beads for each guest and an additional black fabric flower for each female guest. Wrap the beads around the napkins. That's it for the male guests. For an added embellishment, hot-glue a black flower to the beaded front for female guests. To individualize, use a different black bloom for each guest.

Place Cards: Inject a stroke of red with playing card place cards. Simply glue a row of three plastic dice together to make a front and back base (two rows of three per place card). Insert a playing card upright between the two rows of dice, glue it all together, and write the guest's name on top with a red or black marker.

Tangerine Teriyaki Ribs

- 3 racks pork baby back ribs
- 2 cups hickory chips soaked in water at least 1 hour
- 2 packets (1.06 ounces each) ginger teriyaki marinade mix, *McCormick® Grill Mates®*
- 3 cups tangerine juice, divided, *Harvest®*
- 1 cup barbecue sauce, *KC Masterpiece®*

1. Rinse ribs with cold water and pat dry. Remove thin membrane from the back of ribs. Place ribs in a large shallow pan and set aside.

2. In a bowl, combine 2 cups tangerine juice and both packets of ginger teriyaki mix. Pour marinade mixture over ribs. Cover and let marinate in the refrigerator for 1 to 3 hours.

3. Set up grill for indirect cooking over medium heat (no heat source directly under ribs). Remove ribs from refrigerator and allow to come up to room temperature (about 30 minutes).

4. Remove ribs from marinade mixture, but do not discard marinade. Place ribs in rib rack over drip pan on hot grill. Add a handful of hickory chips to the smoke box or each pile of hot coals. Cover grill. Rotate ribs around rack every 30 minutes. If using charcoal, add 10 briquettes to each pile of coals and another handful of soaked hickory chips every hour. Cook 2 to 2½ hours.

5. While ribs are cooking, make sauce by first adding rib marinade to a saucepan. Bring to a boil for 5 minutes over high heat. Reduce heat to medium and add remaining cup of tangerine juice and barbecue sauce. Simmer 10 minutes; remove from heat.

6. About 20 minutes before ribs are done, remove ribs from rib rack and lay, meat sides down, on grill. Generously brush with sauce and pile ribs in center of grill over drip pan. Cover and cook 10 minutes. Turn ribs; brush on more sauce and again move ribs to center of grill. Cook an additional 10 minutes.

7. Cut into portions and serve hot with sauce on the side. Makes 4 servings.

Indoor method: Prepare and marinate ribs as directed. Preheat oven to 350 degrees F. Remove ribs from marinade, reserving marinade, and place meat sides up on rack in a shallow roasting pan. Tightly cover with foil. Bake in preheated oven for 1 hour. While ribs are baking, make sauce as directed. Remove ribs from oven and carefully drain fat from roasting pan. Continue baking ribs, uncovered, for 30 to 45 minutes more or until tender, turning and brushing occasionally with sauce.

Talk-of-the-Town New York Strip

- 4 New York strip steaks
- ¾ cup dry sherry, *Christian Brothers®*
- ¼ cup canola oil, *Wesson®*
- ¼ cup soy sauce, *Kikkoman®*
- 2 tablespoons lime juice, *ReaLime®*
- 2 tablespoons Thai seasoning, *Spice Islands®*

1. Rinse steaks under cold water and pat dry. Put steaks in a zip-top plastic bag and add remaining ingredients. Gently massage bag to combine ingredients. Marinate in refrigerator for 1 to 3 hours.

2. Set up grill for direct cooking over high heat. Oil grate when ready to start cooking. Remove steaks from refrigerator; let come to room temperature (approximately 20 to 30 minutes).

3. Remove steaks from marinade; discard marinade. Place steaks on hot oiled grill and cook for 6 to 8 minutes per side for medium doneness.

4. Transfer steaks to a platter and let rest 5 minutes before serving. Makes 4 servings.

Family Days

For me, food is indelibly linked to family. Every time I frost a cake, memories of my grandma guide my hand. Picking out fresh berries in the market reminds me of picking berries with my sisters in that sticky-sweet berry patch beside our childhood home. Whenever I flip a burger on my gas grill, I experience a whoosh of nostalgia—just like the whoosh of flames when my uncle lit the charcoal all those summer Sundays ago. We live in the age of speed dial. In the rush to go more and do more in less and less time, the family meal has become expendable. A shame, really, because while meals are short, the memories last a lifetime. Semi-Homemade® gives you the best of both worlds—meals cooked fast so you can linger longer with the ones you love.

This chapter is a medley of moods, offering day after day of thematic tablescapes that make food and cocktails—for the adults—part of the mix. Just for fun, pair Sandra's Shortcake and Beer Lemonade with a cowboy boot centerpiece and have a Hoedown. R&R is the Weekend Way, so serve up shells and serenity with Blue Cabo Martinis and Lime Cream Meringues. Postgame, team playful accents with Aunt Sandy's Cherry Sponge Cake and fruity cocktails and incite Sport Mania at home.

We choose our food, we choose our friends, but our family is a gift given from God for life. So set the table, pour the drinks, and gather them close. It's family time, and you'll all be the richer for sharing it.

Aunt Sandy holds Scott and Bryce's catch-of-the-day on a fishing camp-out.

JASON

Gone Fishing

Camping with the family! Why not make it a party, with a palette of river greens and the catch of the day setting the stage for a family meal, a reunion, a birthday, or even a college-bound send-off with the whole family savoring a slice of time together? This summertime gathering is easy and relaxing, with a sporty tablescape that captures the feel of the great outdoors, hook, line, and sinker. The foundation is a windowpane check cloth in a soft celery, set with stacked green graniteware and splashes of silver that glint in the sun. No hemming necessary for the fabric table covering—the gently fringed bottom is appropriately rustic. Pale green grapes and apples make munchies decor, arranged in glass compotes that bookend the tabletop. Even those who can't catch fish will love to eat them when the fish du jour is Trout Ciabatta, made campfire chic with pesto artichoke spread on a chewy baguette. Elegant Amaretto Peaches grill up gorgeous, topped with creamy clouds of Mascarpone cheese and slivered almonds. River Run Cocktails keep to the theme with a fresh mint garnish plucked right from the centerpiece. Use fishing wire to dangle a lure from a green straw (watch that hook!) and you'll be all set to reel in some fun.

Accent Pieces: Silver and glass add sparkle, even when you're "roughing it" outdoors. Function and fashion go hand in hand. Tin camping lanterns add mood lighting and illuminate a dusky path with green candles inside. Galvanized flowerpot saucers become chargers and drink trays. Their steel color recalls those old camping mess kits—and even better, they keep things portable so you can pick up your place setting and move around. A galvanized tub serves iced beverages in green glass bottles that mirror the green drink glasses. A silver bucket holds utensils. **Music:** Upbeat summer tunes like The Beach Boys: *Sounds of Summer* or *The Best of Van Halen, Vol. 1,* top the music menu.

Centerpiece: Masses of fresh, fragrant herbs are breathtakingly beautiful arranged in a footed fishbowl compote. Line the bottom with green grapes, covered with water. Arrange a garden of bushy herbs such as lavender, mint, sage, rosemary, and thyme, layering them so the centerpiece has height. The color brightens the tablescape, and the water keeps the herbs fresh.

Place Card Favors: Napkin rings and place cards are one and the same. Make them by tying a plastic fishing lure around a green-and-white striped napkin with clear fishing line. The place cards are round hangtags from the office supply store, personalized with each guest's name and strung on the lures. Guests can take them home to try on their next fishing trip.

Fashion: Don't dress for dinner—a white cotton t-shirt with a lace cotton cami is cool, calm, and crisply coordinated.

Trout Ciabatta

- **2 pounds trout, cleaned, heads and tails removed**
- **1 cup olive oil and vinegar salad dressing, *Newman's Own*®**
- **3 tablespoons orange juice concentrate, *Minute Maid*®**
- **1 tablespoon fines herbes, *Spice Islands*®**
- **1 teaspoon red pepper flakes, *Spice Islands* ®**
- **1 cup lemon pesto artichoke spread, *Delallo*®**
- **1 loaf (19-ounce) ciabatta bread**
- **2 cups spring salad mix, *Fresh Express*®**
- **2 tomatoes, sliced**
- **½ small onion, thinly sliced**

1. Place cleaned trout in a large zip-top plastic bag; set aside. Stir together salad dressing, orange juice concentrate, herbs, and red pepper flakes. Pour into bag with fish. Squeeze air from bag and seal. Marinate in the refrigerator 1 to 2 hours.

2. Remove fish from marinade and discard marinade. Place fish on grill, flesh sides down, and cook 3 to 4 minutes per side. Remove and set aside. Slice ciabatta bread horizontally and toast on grill. Remove and slather both sides with artichoke spread. Carefully pull skin from trout fillets (bones should come up with skin). Assemble sandwiches with salad mix, tomatoes, and onions; cut into serving-size pieces. Makes 6 servings.

Amaretto Peaches

- **6 peaches, halved**
- **½ cup amaretto liqueur**
- **2 tablespoons orange juice concentrate, *Minute Maid*®**
- **6 whole cloves, *McCormick*®**
- **1 container (8-ounce) mascarpone, softened, *Cantare*®**
- **½ cup slivered almonds, toasted, *Planters*®**

1. Place halved peaches in a large zip-top plastic bag; set aside. Stir together amaretto, orange juice concentrate, and cloves. Pour into zip-top bag with peaches. Marinate in refrigerator for 1 to 4 hours.

2. Meanwhile set up grill for direct grilling. Grill peaches directly over medium heat for 5 to 8 minutes or until peaches begin to brown and soften. Remove peaches from grill and cool slightly.

3. Stir together mascarpone and ¼ cup almonds. Refrigerate until ready to use. Fill peaches with almond mascarpone cream and garnish with remaining almonds. Makes 6 servings.

River Run Cocktail

- **3 fresh mint leaves**
- **Crushed ice**
- **½ lime, juiced**
- **1 bottle beer, *Corona*®**
- **Fresh mint sprig, for garnish**

1. Place mint leaves in bottom of highball glass. Fill with crushed ice. Add lime juice and stir. Add beer. Garnish with fresh mint sprig. Makes 1 drink.

GO
GO
WIN

Sport Mania

As "Aunt Sandy" to five nephews and three nieces, I have become a huge fan of sports, whether they're on the field or on the table. Throwing a sports-theme party is just one more way to have fun. Invite your kids' teammates over after a big game, host a victory celebration, or toast the team, no matter the score. Or maybe it's your or your spouse's team that's ready to play. Either way, America's favorite colors are just the ticket for America's favorite pastime, so bring out those reds, whites, and blues. Play out the patriotic palette with red and blue dishes, topped with napkins matched to the tablecloth. Just roll the napkins picnic style and secure with wristbands embellished with sports-themed decals used as napkin rings. A picnic plaid tablecovering is appropriately outdoorsy, whether you set up inside or out. Find a fabric you like, cut it to fit, and spread it on. Why hem? Those frayed edges only add to the charm. A little comfort food is just what the menu needs, so pour some fruity red punch, then finish up with Aunt Sandy's Cherry Sponge Cake. It's pretty enough for a centerpiece. Top each serving with a scoop of ice cream and it'll score major points. When dessert's done, use the place cards to catch some fun out back.

Accent Pieces: A customized photo frame becomes a tabletop montage when accessorized with baseball ornaments. To make the photo frame, use 3-M Spray Mount® adhesive to cover the frame's cardboard backing with a fabric matching your tablecloth. Spray-Mount® your photo centered on the fabric; let dry and reassemble the frame. **Place Cards:** This easy-on-the-eye tablescape makes good use of things you may already have. "Autographed" baseballs pinch-hit as place cards when you personalize them with your guests' names.

GO
GO
WIN

Centerpiece: "Go" and "Win" pennants spell "fun" arranged in a decorative cookie jar football helmet with red, white, and blue pompoms. The bottom of the helmet is a candy dish filled with red M&M's®. It's all store bought, so you can pull it together in minutes.

Favors: A baseball-theme goodie box makes a colorful table accessory or send it home with guests as a favor. To make, spray paint an unfinished wooden box white. After it dries, apply 3-M Spray Mount® adhesive to fabric that matches the tablecloth and wrap it around the bottom of the box. Hot-glue a narrow red grosgrain ribbon around the top of the base and use a red marker to add baseball stitching to the lid. Fill the box with party recipes for adults; for the kids, fill with baseball cards, energy bars, or candies.

Food and Drink: Pretty glass bowls filled with red and blue almonds or M&M's® turn snacks into grab-and-go table decor.

Music: Sing "Take Me Out to the Ballgame" at least once.

Watermelon Punch: With a knife, shave off the stem end of a 4-pound watermelon just enough so that it sits flat. Cut the top off the watermelon, about 3 inches down. Scoop out half of the watermelon with a melon baller. Set aside melon balls. Scoop out remaining watermelon, leaving the rind bowl. This will be your punch bowl. Transfer scooped-out melon (not the melon balls) to a blender and puree (may be done in batches). Combine pureed melon, 2 cups Sprite®, 1 cup Hawaiian Punch®, and melon balls in watermelon bowl.

Aunt Sandy's Cherry Sponge Cake

1 10-ounce purchased sponge cake
1 can (21-ounce) cherry pie filling, *Comstock*®
1 cup frozen cherries, thawed, *Dole*®
1 teaspoon almond extract
Vanilla ice cream (optional)

1. Place sponge cake round on a serving platter or plate. Set aside.

2. In a saucepan over medium-high heat combine cherry pie filling, frozen cherries, and almond extract. Bring cherry mixture to boil. Reduce heat and simmer for 5 minutes. Cool slightly.

3. Pour cherry mixture over top of sponge cake. Serve with a scoop of vanilla ice cream, if desired. Makes 10 servings.

Come Sail Away

"Come sail away, come sail away, come sail away with me..." The tempting lyrics from that '70s Styx song are invitation enough for a party, whether you're celebrating a birthday, bon voyage, or just for fun. Forget the weather and bring the festivities inside. Get the table in the mood with a navigational print tablecloth in a regatta of reds, blues, and whites that makes a shipshape backdrop for a stacked place setting: folded blue and white napkins and wavy white salad plates atop Navy blue dinner plates, with sea-blue Lucite®-handled silverware on the side. Nautical accents abound, from woven place mats that resemble coiled rope to the sailboat and lighthouse centerpiece (purchased right from the craft store and spray painted blue and white). Landlubbers will love the Sautéed Bananas, anchored with an oatmeal cookie and a captain's wheel. All hands on deck! The Cranberry Margaritas will transport you to a state of bliss, especially when you pour on the ambience with Jimmy Buffett's *Songs You Know by Heart* or *Reggae Best* by Bob Marley and the Wailers. Be sure to make some of the cocktails Shirley Temples so the kids can partake. Serve them in tall, summery glasses, garnished with a lime wedge and a blue straw, and you can all sip in style.

Place Cards: Adirondack chair place cards look just beachy embellished with captain's wheels and blue netting. Buy an Adirondack chair photo frame and hot-glue nautical scrapbooking decals to it. Spray paint it to match your party colors. Pen each guest's name on a sheet of paper and put it in the photo slot. **Window Treatment:** Simply wrap an extra length of your tablecloth fabric across the window and thumbtack it in place with accenting fabric swags; tack swags in a flag-like fashion. Dangle wooden anchors from the swags with fishing line and arrange accents on the counter. **Favors:** Guests will find a take-home recipe box fun. Hot-glue raw wood mini lighthouses across the bottom of a wooden recipe box, paint white and let dry. Paint blue bands on the top and bottom of the lighthouses, let dry. Hot-glue tiny sailboats to the lid and a shell "knob" to the front. Glue a party recipe to a blue card stock tag and attach it to the box with a shoelace or rope twine.

Cranberry Margarita

1½ shots tequila, *Jose Cuervo*®
1 shot cranberry juice, *Ocean Spray*®
¼ cup whole cranberry sauce, *Ocean Spray*®
½ shot orange liqueur, *Cointreau*®
10 ice cubes
Dried cranberries, for garnish
Lime wedge, for garnish

1. Combine all ingredients, except dried cranberries and lime wedge, in blender. Blend on HIGH until smooth. Serve in a margarita glass. Garnish with dried cranberries and a lime wedge. Makes 1 drink.

Sautéed Bananas

½ stick (¼ cup) butter
4 medium bananas, underripe, cut diagonally into ½-inch slices
¼ cup dark rum, *Myer's*®
3 tablespoons packed brown sugar
¼ teaspoon ground cinnamon, *McCormick*®
1 pint vanilla bean ice cream, *Häagen-Dazs*®
Purchased oatmeal cookies

1. In a large skillet, over medium-high heat, melt butter. Add bananas to butter; cook for 1 minute. Stir in rum, brown sugar, and cinnamon. Simmer for 3 to 4 minutes.

2. Scoop ice cream into four dessert dishes. Top with bananas and syrup. Serve with oatmeal cookies. Makes 4 servings.

Floral Blooms

Here comes the sun! Hothouse hues and perky perennials create a sunny mood for any party, whether it's a bridal shower, birthday, or Mother's Day. When the setting is this bewitching, "I just want to throw a party" is excuse enough. This gathering is all about color and flowers—so turn to your garden, grocery, or even the craft store for flowers in summer's hottest shades. Can't find Gerbera daisies? Pick lilies, daffodils, tulips, or a merry mix. A lemon yellow tablecloth lays the groundwork for citrus stripes, started with a five-minute table scarf and carried through to the plates. Do as I did and buy a square yard of fabric and turn the edges under with double-stick tape. Striped dishes play off the pattern of the table scarf, while blue and green Lucite®-handled silverware ties into the blue base of the polka dot glasses. Red and yellow daisy topiaries flanking the window are accent pieces that set the room abloom. The menu starts with Bacon-Wrapped Artichoke Hearts, an appetizer so decadent and delicious, it's hard to believe it has only two ingredients! Citrusy desserts are clearly part of the palette. Spice up a store-bought cheesecake with fresh oranges, marmalade, orange juice, and Cointreau® and you've got one hot party.

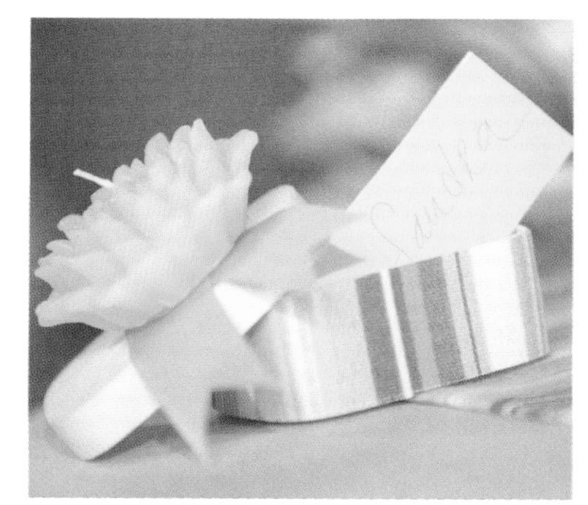

Centerpiece: Here, brilliant Gerbera daisies bloom in a chip and dip bowl. Fit floral foam in the bottom bowl, clip the stems of faux daisies, and arrange them so the heads spill over the sides. Place a decorative candle in the dip bowl.

Place Cards: To make this trinket box, hot-glue fabric matching the table scarf to the base of a plain craft store box. Hot-glue a "V" of yellow ribbon to the lid and a candle to the ribbon. Write the guest's name on yellow card stock.

Favors: Paint an unfinished wooden recipe box green and glue a 1½-inch yellow ribbon around the top. Glue an additional ribbon-width length of fabric that matches the table scarf around the top of the lid. Hot-glue faux Gerbera daisy heads onto the top of the box.

Bacon-Wrapped Artichoke Hearts

1 **jar (12-ounce) marinated artichoke heart quarters, *Luna Rossa*®**
9 **slices bacon, cut in half, *Oscar Mayer*®**

1. Preheat oven to 425 degrees F. Line baking sheet with aluminum foil. Drain artichoke heart quarters, reserving liquid. Wrap each artichoke heart quarter with a half-slice bacon. Secure with a toothpick.

2. Place on baking sheet. Drizzle with reserved liquid from artichokes. Roast in preheated oven for 12 to 15 minutes or until bacon is cooked through. Makes 4 servings.

Orange-Spiced Cheesecake

1 **box (17-ounce) frozen cheesecake, (not New York-style), *Sara Lee*®**
1/3 **cup orange marmalade, *Smucker's*®**
2 **tablespoons orange liqueur, *Cointreau*®**
1 **tablespoon frozen orange juice concentrate, *Minute Maid*®**
1/4 **teaspoon five-spice powder, *McCormick*®**
1 **orange,* sliced**

1. Cut cheesecake into quarters and let stand at room temperature for at least 15 minutes.

2. In a large saucepan, over medium-high heat, combine marmalade, orange liqueur, frozen orange juice concentrate, and five-spice powder. Simmer until orange juice concentrate is melted. Add orange slices. Simmer about 10 minutes or until thick and syrupy. Reduce heat; keep warm.

3. To serve, spoon warm orange mixture over cheesecake slices. Makes 4 servings.

***Note**: Use blood oranges in the winter season for a festive touch.

Orange Kahlúa® Coffee

1 1/2 **shots coffee liqueur, *Kahlúa*®**
1 **shot mandarin orange vodka, *Absolut*®**
Hot brewed coffee
Frozen whipped topping, thawed, *Cool Whip*®

1. In a coffee glass or mug, combine coffee liqueur and vodka. Fill coffee glass or mug with coffee. Float a spoonful of whipped topping on top. Serve hot. Makes 1 drink.

A Fall Feast

The air turns crisp, leaves fall from trees, and pumpkins appear on porches. Fall is here—and I love every minute of it. What a glorious time of year and what a perfect excuse to throw a party! Invite the whole crew over to cheer your team to victory, host a pumpkin-carving contest, or have game night chez vous. Regardless of the reason, celebrate all that's fall by decorating your tablescape in earthy tones: rich browns, quiet ambers, and velvety reds. A rust and cream fabric table covering captures the subdued side of fall with a rustic woven pattern that makes a soft backdrop for textured pottery in cocoas and creams. (Don't bother to hem the tablecloth—fringed edges add rustic appeal.) Earthenware plates are made food safe with clear glass plates on top; they also top vases to become serving pedestals. Even the menu shows off the colors of the season. Red Velvet Bars are a delicious crimson, with cream cheese frosting that deepens the red. Stack them to showcase their beauty, then rustle up some Cowgirl Coolers, punched up with fresh ginger. An ambery ale color, they're lovely served in Pilsner glasses with slices of lime and sprigs of mint.

Centerpiece: A handmade vase looks fresh from the kiln. Its red-brown hue sets off stems of faux fall berries. Flank the vase with a trio of marbled pillar candles that add interest with staggered heights. **Place Settings:** Stacks of natural-tone napkins are topped with a rolled napkin tied with sprigs of berries—a lovely link to the tablecloth and centerpiece. **Place Cards:** Start with small manila envelopes from the office supply store. Fold the bottom up to make a pocket, then slip a gold place card inside. **Accent Pieces:** A cut out decorative vase candleholder casts twinkly light.

Cowgirl Coolers

- 1 2-inch piece fresh ginger, sliced
- 2 cups water
- 1 can (12-ounce) frozen concentrated lemonade, thawed, *Minute Maid®*
- 4½ cups ginger ale, *Canada Dry®*
- 1½ cups vodka, *Absolut®*
- Ice cubes
- 1 lime, sliced, for garnish

1. In a small saucepan, bring sliced ginger and water to a boil. Remove from heat and steep for 20 minutes. Strain and reserve liquid.

2. In a large pitcher, stir to combine lemonade concentrate, ginger water, ginger ale, and vodka.

3. Serve over ice and garnish with lime slice. Makes 12 drinks.

Red Velvet Bars

- 1 package (18.25-ounce) German chocolate cake mix, *Betty Crocker®*
- 1 stick butter, softened
- 1 egg
- 1 ounce red food coloring, *McCormick®*
- 2 packages (8 ounces each) cream cheese, softened, *Philadelphia®*
- ½ cup sugar
- 2 eggs
- 1 teaspoon vanilla extract, *McCormick®*

1. Preheat oven to 350 degrees F. Spray a 9×13-inch foil pan with cooking spray; set aside.

2. In a large mixing bowl, with an electric mixer on low speed, beat cake mix, butter, egg, and food coloring until combined.

3. Press cake mixture into prepared pan; set aside.

4. In a medium mixing bowl, beat cream cheese and sugar on medium speed until creamy. Add eggs and vanilla; beat to combine.

5. Spread cream cheese mixture over cake layer.

6. Bake in preheated oven for 40 to 45 minutes or until bars just begin to pull away from sides. Cool completely before cutting. Makes 24 bars.

Under the Sea

Sparkling, mesmerizing, awe inspiring—the words to describe the ocean's majesty are infinite, just like the possibilities for this stunning table. Call on its *Blue Hawaii* setting for a bon voyage, an "I need a vacation" party, or après trip to show off those photos. It's all about the contrast of color and the play of light—aquamarine waves capped by foamy white, the quicksilver of fish scales, bits of cobalt, and bottle green sea glass nestled in sugary sand. Jewel tones crown the table, from glasses that flash like diamonds to blue topaz candle globes to the coral reef centerpiece that comes alive with beaded accents—all grounded by table coverings layered blue atop white. Like the table, the menu is an equal blend of easygoing and elegant, starting with spiced-up Avocado Shrimp you can buy precooked, peeled, and deveined to make it easy on the host. Team the shrimp with gorgeous Blue Seafoam cocktails, made as blue as the waves with fresh blueberries that float, suspended in a sea of flavored vodka and blue curaço. Set it all up in your living room or on the back porch, whenever you're longing to be miles away—if only in spirit.

Accent Pieces: The flicker of candlelight is the only accent you'll need. Mottled pale blue and green pillar candles rest on rounds of faux white disk coral, their sand-strewn texture playing off the ridged coral to add interest. Buy dripless candles and hot-glue them in place to avoid accidents.

Place Settings: The soft scallops of oysterlike plates put food on the half shell, with sea blue napkins slipped casually between. Blue Lucite®-handled silverware and roly-poly drink glasses recall the lapping of waves. Tilting and rolling (but not spilling), the glasses add a fun note, reminiscent of childhood days at the shore. Find them at home stores or online.

Centerpiece: Color, texture, height—this stunning centerpiece has them all. Blue-greens ripple, undulate, and shimmer, traversing a spectrum from sapphire to emerald as they catch the light. Arrange two large pieces of faux white disk coral and 2 to 3 smaller disk corals (found in the aquarium section of most pet stores) to make the "reef." Hot-glue 7 to 9 beaded or glittered seahorse and starfish ornaments around the coral, then scatter a few pearlescent balls around the base to finish.

Accent Pieces: Blue globes pair frosted and ribbed glass with white pillar candles to cast a warm glow over the tabletop. Anchor the candles in sand, then scatter the candle bowls around the tabletop or hang from candle stands to create a chandelier effect.

Place Card Favors: Extra starfish ornaments from the centerpiece make the base for the takeaway place card. The name card is two dolphin-shape cutouts—one blue, one white—slotted together for a two-tone effect. Buy these ready-made if you can, or use a cookie cutter or template to trace the design onto two colors of cardstock. Cut them out, make small slits to slot them together—white atop blue—and pen the guest's name on the white dolphin with blue ink. Cut another small slit in the top of the ornament base and insert the slotted cards to finish the place card.

Music: Mood music like *Stardust Melody* by Hoagy Carmichael adds to the ambience in a laid-back way.

Fashion: My ocean blue linen shirt layered over warm-weather whites captures that vacation carefree mood.

Avocado Shrimp

- **8 ounces cooked, peeled, and deveined bay or other shrimp**
- **½ cup refrigerated pico de gallo salsa**
- **2 tablespoons bottled lime juice, *ReaLime*®**
- **2 tablespoons finely chopped fresh cilantro**
- **1 avocado, diced**
- **Salt and ground black pepper**

1. In a medium bowl, combine shrimp, salsa, lime juice, and cilantro. Let stand for 5 to 10 minutes.

2. Add avocado; toss to combine. Season to taste with salt and pepper. Makes 4 servings.

Blue Seafoam

- **Ice cubes**
- **1½ parts of blueberry vodka, *Stoli*®**
- **1½ parts of vanilla vodka, *Stoli*®**
- **Splash *Blue Curacao*®**
- **Blueberries, for garnish**

1. Fill a cocktail shaker with ice cubes. Add all ingredients, except blueberry garnish, and shake well.

2. Pour into a highball glass and garnish with fresh blueberries. Makes 1 drink.

Hoedown

Don that cowboy hat, rustle up a bandana, and put on some good ole country music to get those boots a'tappin'! It's high time for a Hoedown, and your house is just the place to have one. Round up the family or invite your citified friends over and show them what it's like to be a cowgirl (or boy)—for a day, anyway. Swap root beer for beer and you've got the perfect party for a boy's birthday. Keep the color scheme to rustic barn reds and browns, accented with distressed metals, and the setting becomes pure country. A charming Old West runner lays the groundwork for Western accessories, while the maroon undercloth sets the pace for the tablescape's reds. The menu is drinks and desserts, but it can easily be expanded. (How 'bout BBQ ribs on the grill and tubs of baked beans and coleslaw, straight from the deli?) First up is Beer Lemonade, light and refreshing, with a combination of flavors that's totally unexpected. Follow with Sandra's Shortcake, so easy and so delicious everyone will be asking for seconds and thirds.

Place Cards: A drinkable place card—how cool is that! To make, slip a longneck bottle of beer into a mug. Write the guest's name on a piece of red cardstock, embellished with Western-style scrapbooking stickers like a boot and a star. Hole-punch one end of the place card and slip a leather shoelace through the hole. Add a wood-handled beer opener and knot the ends, then drape necklace style over the beer bottle.

DENISE
JEFF
SANDRA

Place Settings: It all starts with the place mat, a piece of rope wound into a coil and hot-glued in place. The plates are a dead ringer in hemp-color ceramic with a textured rope border. Red cloth napkins are folded kerchief-style and clipped in back with a mini clothespin. Atop the stacked plates, they add mid level height to the table.

Centerpiece: Guests will get a kick out of this "authentic" centerpiece—a glossy cowboy boot filled with dried grasses. Just pick up an old boot at a secondhand store (or take one from your closet) and shine it up with liquid resin or lacquer. After it dries, fill it with wheat stalks and dried grasses to make a fun floral alternative.

Accent Pieces: Footed glass bowls display red pears and apples. An old oiled-leather saddlebag filled with fragrant basil and wine bottles follows suit. Patinaed copper cups moonlight as candleholders. Anchor the candles with sand, salt, or sugar.

Food and Drink: A "Beer Topiary" is a fun way to dispense refreshment. Slide bottles of beer—or lemonade—into a coppery wine rack to create a self-serve beverage bar. Take dessert to new heights by stacking dinner plates filled with shortcakes into tiers; hammered tin canisters turned upside down form the base of the pedestal.

Favors: Yippee! This little takeaway is easy. Just computer-print a party recipe and hot-glue it to the back of a vintage cowboy-theme postcard, then tuck one under each napkin. Guests will remember your party when they re-create the dish at home.

Music: Start the toe-tappin' by spinning Lyle Lovett's *Live in Texas*.

Beer Lemonade

Crushed ice
¼ cup lemonade
1 bottle beer, ***Corona®***
Lemon slice, for garnish

1. Fill a highball glass with crushed ice. Add lemonade and stir. Add beer. Garnish with lemon slice. Makes 1 drink.

Sandra's Shortcake

1 can (16.3-ounce) biscuits, ***Pillsbury® Grands! Southern Style***
2 pints fresh strawberries, quartered
¾ cup sugar, divided
1 teaspoon cinnamon, ***McCormick®***
1 container (8-ounce) frozen whipped topping, thawed, ***Cool Whip®***
1 cup dairy sour cream, ***Knudson®***
Whole strawberries, for garnish

1. Preheat oven to 350 degrees F. Unroll southern style biscuit can. Place on baking sheet and bake according to package directions.

2. In a medium bowl, combine the strawberries and ½ cup sugar. Let stand for 1 hour to meld flavors.

3. In a small bowl, combine ¼ cup sugar and cinnamon. Remove biscuits from oven; split the biscuits and dredge in cinnamon sugar; place biscuit bottoms on serving plate. Top biscuits with the quartered strawberries.

4. Place thawed whipped topping in a bowl and fold in the sour cream. Top shortcake with a dollop of whipped topping mixture. Add biscuit top. Add more whipped topping mixture and garnish with whole strawberries. Makes 8 servings.

Weekend Way

What is it about the call of the sea? Its colors soothe us, its sounds relax us, and the shells washed from its depths become treasures we gather and claim as our own. It is at the same time rejuvenating and relaxing, calming and inspiring, cool yet warm. To capture this mood at a party is to guarantee your guests a good time. Set on the beach with waves lapping against the sand and a warm breeze ruffling the table linens, the scene is unpretentiously elegant. Make it an intimate gathering—a birthday celebration for a spouse, an engagement party, a milestone anniversary. The palette draws from the spunkier shades of blues—teals, turquoises, and aquamarines—softened with white candles and billowing white sheering draped from bamboo poles to make a grand entrance. Seating is simple—a low folding table set on the sand and covered with a teal cloth, surrounded by tufted floor cushions with seawater stripes. The menu is beautifully beachy. Begin with Blue Cabo Martinis and clams served in sand buckets. (It is a celebration, after all.) Dessert is dreamy white meringues with lighter-than-air lime filling. And while the sea is undeniably a scene-stealer, you can always re-create the table setting at home to tide you over until your next weekend away.

Accent Pieces: Mood lighting is a must, and candles keep it soft and inviting. Fill frosted blue glass tumblers halfway with sand—enough to anchor the elegant white tapers. A deep Caribbean blue decanter and large pieces of white coral play up the shimmering color of Blue Cabo Martinis, inspired by the ever-changing colors of the sea.

Place Settings: Every element springs from the sea, making coordination effortless. Place mats are faux mother of pearl. The scalloped edges of the white plates mimic waves. Napkins with ocean blue stripes are ensconced in starfish napkin rings. They're easy to make—just hot-glue a white starfish to a plain white napkin ring.

Centerpiece: Simplicity has never been more irresistible. Two glass cylinder vases—one slightly taller than the other —are filled with a hodgepodge of seashells and coral. A few inches of sand in the bottom adds to the ambience and prevents the shells from breaking when you drop them in. You can buy bags of shells at craft stores or pull from your own collection for sentimental value.

Place Card Favors: A seashell picture frame announces the gathering. You can include takeaway favors that double as place cards. Simply buy miniature seashell frames, slip a name card in the photo opening, and set one at each place. Or buy miniature mixed shells and make your own by hot-gluing them around the edges of a ready-made frame. Finish with white cording hot-glued around the edges.

Music: Play up the romance of the beach with *The Very Best of the Drifters* or an album by The Four Tops.

Lime-Cream Meringues

Meringues
- **3 egg whites**
- **½ teaspoon vanilla, *McCormick®***
- **¼ teaspoon cream of tartar**
- **1 cup sugar**

Filling
- **2 cups whipping cream**
- **1 tablespoon sugar**
- **1 tablespoon lime-flavor gelatin, *Jell-O®***

1. Let egg whites stand in a large mixing bowl for 30 minutes. Cover a baking sheet with parchment paper or foil; draw eight 3-inch circles. Add vanilla and the cream of tartar to egg whites. Beat with an electric mixer on medium speed until soft peaks form (tips curl). Add 1 cup sugar, a tablespoon at a time, beating on high speed until very stiff peaks form (tips stand straight) and sugar is almost dissolved.

2. Spread or pipe meringue over circles on paper and shape into shells. Bake in a 300 degree F oven for 30 minutes. Turn oven off; let meringues dry in oven with door closed for at least 1 hour (do not open door). Peel off paper. Store in an airtight container.

3. In a chilled mixing bowl, beat together the whipping cream, the 1 tablespoon sugar, and lime gelatin. Beat just until stiff peaks form. Spoon into a pastry bag or a resealable plastic bag fitted with a star tip. Pipe filling into shells. Makes 8 servings.

Blue Cabo Martini

- **Ice cubes**
- **2 parts tequila, *Jose Cuervo®***
- **1 part blue curaçao, *DeKuyper®***
- **1 tablespoon frozen limeade concentrate, *Minute Maid®***
- **Lemon-lime soda, *Sprite®***

1. Fill a cocktail shaker with ice. Add tequila, curaço, and frozen limeade concentrate. Shake vigorously.

2. Pour into martini glass and top with lemon-lime soda. Makes 1 drink.

Serving Idea: Sand pails double as spectacular shellfish grab-and-go servers.

Place Settings

Place settings are simple when you have a few guidelines. Start with the outside utensils and work your way in. The napkin always goes to the far left, outside of the fork farthest from the plate or centered on the plate, centered or on the plate . Here are the four place settings I use the most when entertaining.

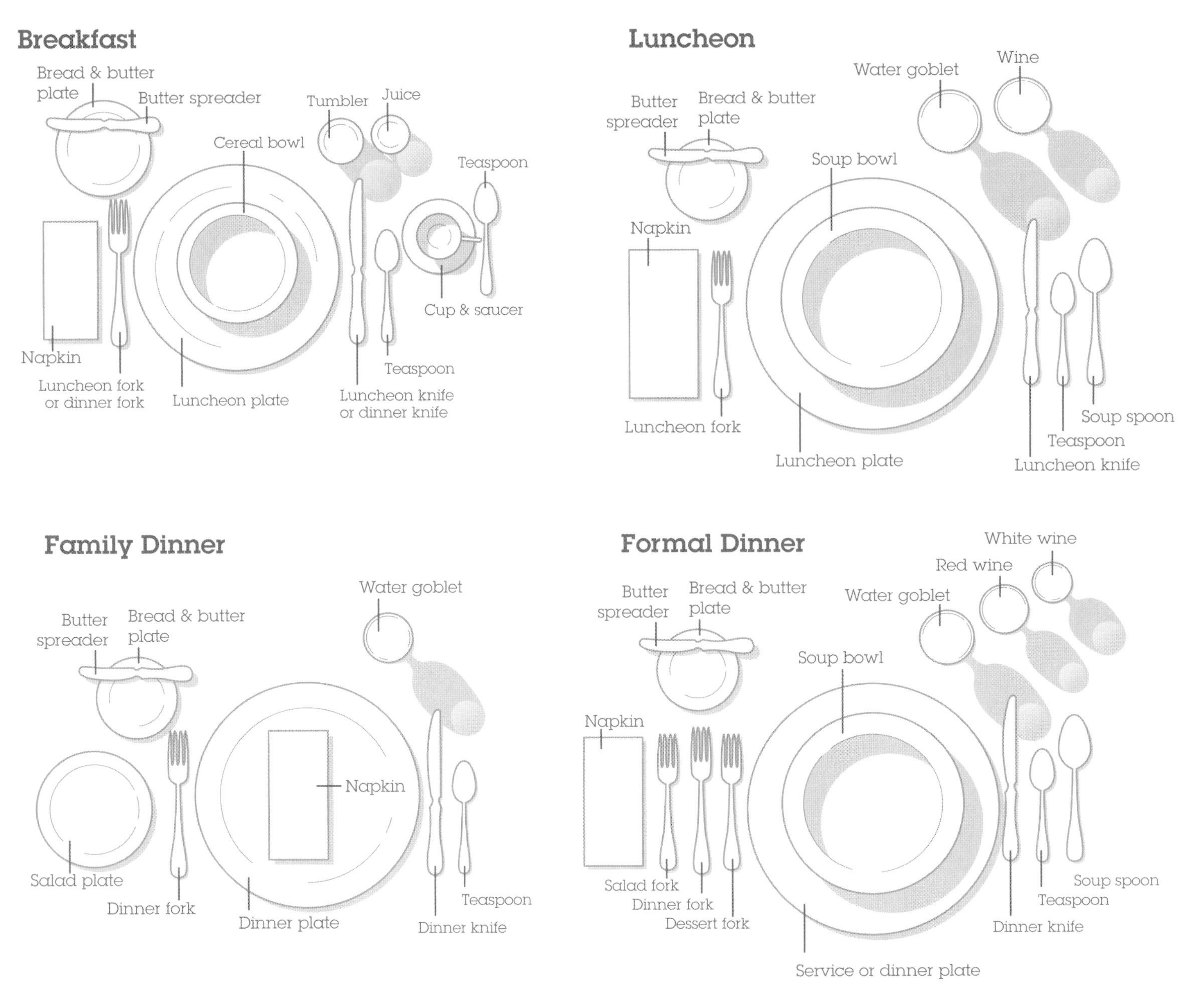

Bird of Paradise

Fold napkin in half, and then half again horizontally.

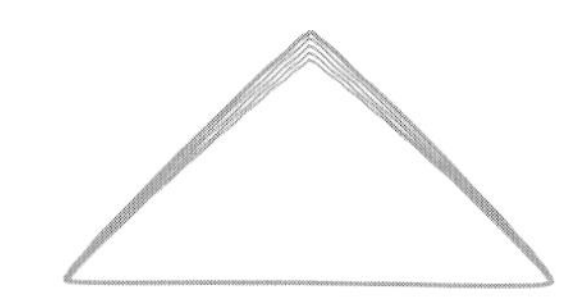

Fold in half diagonally with points on the top and facing up.

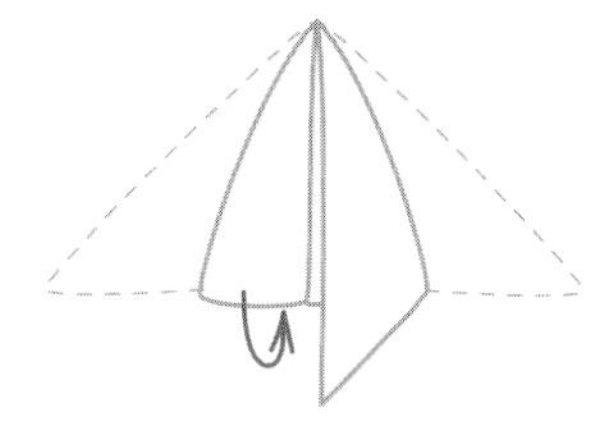

Fold left and right sides down along center line, turning their extended points under.

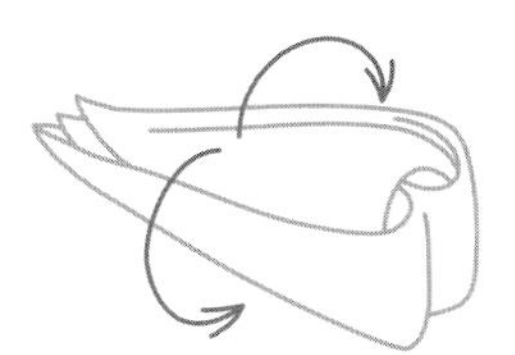

Fold the next layer back and inside, leaving about an inch exposed.

Pull up points and arrange fabric on a surface.

Ice Cream Cone

Start with flat napkin.

Fold in quarters with loose points at top.

Fold the first layer back to the center and tuck inside so it lies flat and forms a pouch.

Fold the next layer back and inside, leaving about an inch exposed.

Fold the next layer back and inside, leaving about an inch exposed.

Turn the whole thing over.

Fold right and left points together so that they overlap forming the "cone."

Flip back over.

The Crown

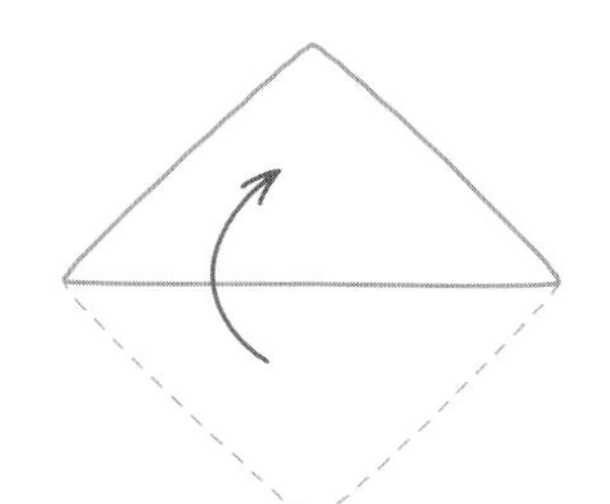

Fold napkin in half diagonally.

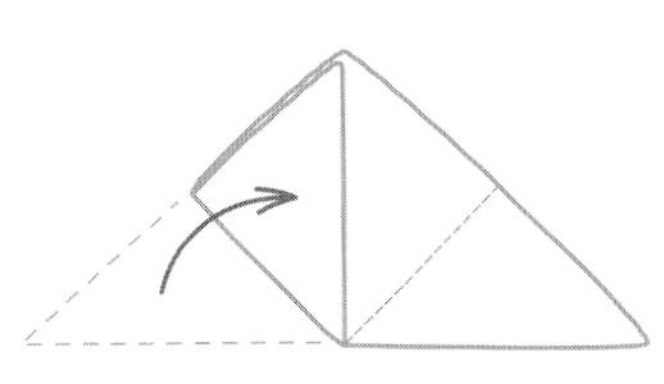

Fold corners to meet at top point.

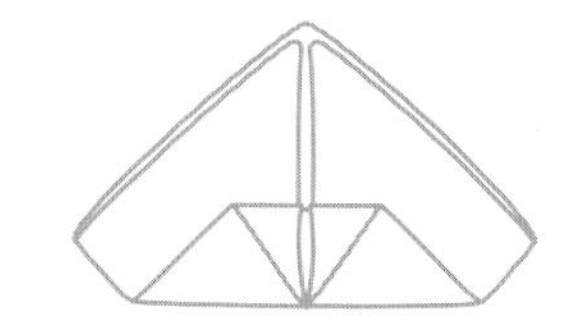

Fold bottom point $^{2}/_{3}$ way to top and fold back onto itself.

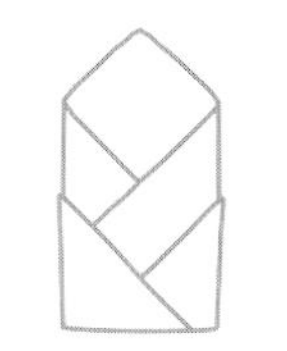

Turn napkin over bringing together. Tuck one into the other.

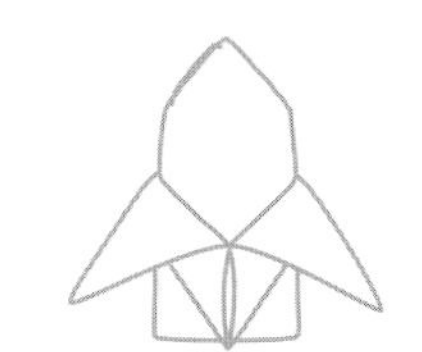

Peel two top corners to make crown. Then open base of fold and stand upright.

The Arum Lily

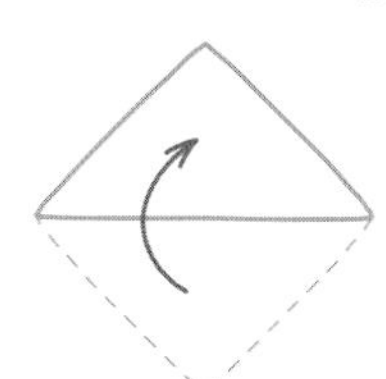

Fold napkin bringing bottom up to top.

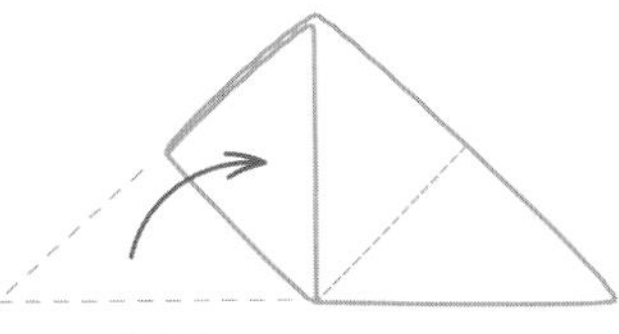

Fold corners to top.

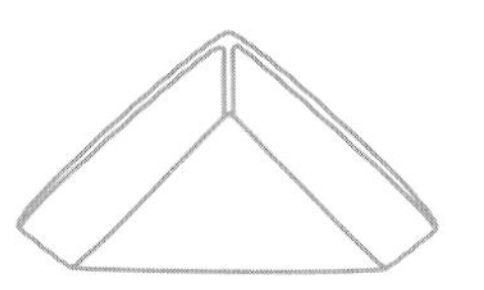

Fold bottom point up to 1 inch below top.

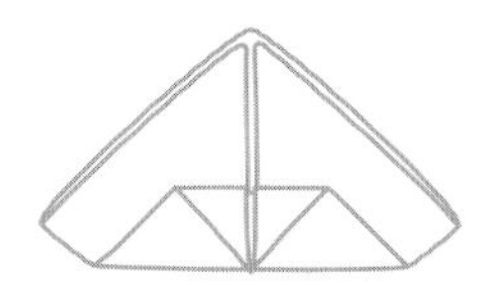

Fold point back onto itself.

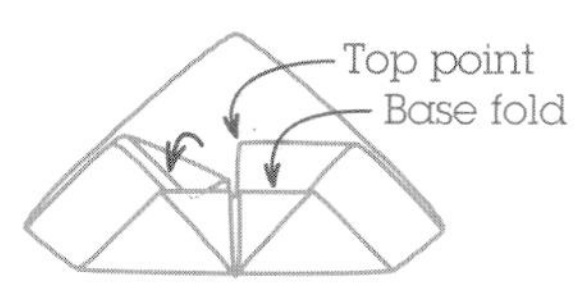

Fold down each of points at top and tuck under edge of folded-up bottom. Fold down one layer of top point and tuck under base fold.

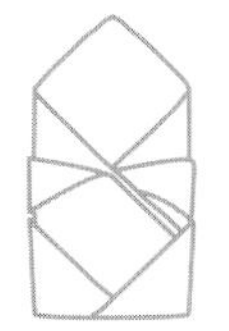

Turn napkin over and tuck left and right sides into each other.

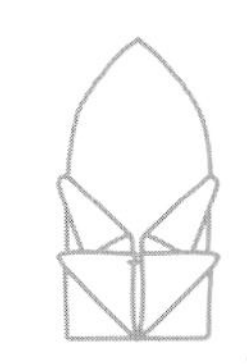

Open base and stand upright.

Alex
Jan
Colleen

Hosting Preparation

When it comes to parties, planning pays off—with a fabulous gathering and a stress-free hostess (that's you).

Getting Started
(1 month ahead for a formal party;
2 weeks ahead for a casual gathering)

__Decide on the date, place, and style of party.
__Make up the guest list.
__Plan the menu.
__For formal parties, mail invitations.
For casual parties, mail invitations or telephone your guests to invite them.
__Decide what table settings, decorations, centerpieces, and music you'll use.
__Make arrangements for any items you'll need to rent or borrow.

Preliminary Preparations
(1 to 2 weeks ahead)

__Telephone any guests who have not responded to your invitations so you can get a definite guest count.
__Do preliminary housecleaning, especially any time-consuming tasks. Make sure all appliances that you'll be using work.
__Compile your grocery shopping list.
__Check that table linens are clean and ready to go.
Decide on tableware and serving pieces.
__Order any special flowers, meats, seafood, or other ingredients you'll need.
__If you're making decorations or centerpieces yourself, now's the time to get started.
__If possible, make some foods ahead and freeze them.

Gearing Up
(2 to 3 days ahead)

__Shop for everything but the most perishable items.
__After you return from shopping, recheck your recipes to make sure you have everything you need.
__Plan your timetable for cooking the foods.
__If possible, make items you can store at room temperature, such as snack mixes, ahead.

24 Hours to Go
(1 day ahead)

__Shop for perishable and last-minute items.
__Reclean the house as necessary.
__Decorate for the party. Prepare an area for coats and umbrellas.
__If possible, arrange and set your table (s) and serving areas.
__Prepare as many recipes and ingredients as possible.
For example, chop vegetables you'll cook as part of a recipe.
__Thaw frozen items. If the items are perishable, thaw them in the refrigerator.
__Decide on your wardrobe.

Let's Party
(1 hour ahead)

__Put all the finishing touches on the meal and tables.
__Clear a spot for placing used dishes as guests finish with them and provide an easily accessible place for garbage.
__Set out cheese and nonperishable appetizers or snacks, if using.
__Get dressed.

As the Doorbell Rings
(5 to 15 minutes ahead)

__Open wine, if serving. Set out remaining appetizers or snacks, if serving.
__Light candles and turn on music, if using.
__Set out cheese and nonperishable appetizers or snacks, if serving.
__Have a cocktail.

Index & Candids

ABCO
CRITICAL SIGNS

Free

Lifestyle web magazine subscription

Just visit
www.semihomemade.com
today to subscribe!

Sign yourself and your friends and family up to the semi-homemaker's club today!

Each online issue is filled with fast, easy how-to projects, simple lifestyle solutions, and an abundance of helpful hints and terrific tips. It's the complete go-to magazine for busy people on-the-move.

tables & settings fashion & beauty ideas home & garden fabulous florals
super suppers perfect parties great gatherings decadent desserts
gifts & giving details wines & music fun favors semi-homemaker's club

semihomemade.com

making life easier, better, and more enjoyable

Semihomemade.com has hundreds of ways to simplify your life—the easy Semi-Homemade way! You'll find fast ways to de-clutter, try your hand at clever crafts, create terrific tablescapes or decorate indoors and out to make your home and garden superb with style.

We're especially proud of our Semi-Homemakers club: a part of semihomemade.com which hosts other semihomemakers just like you. The club community shares ideas to make life easier, better, and more manageable with smart tips and hints allowing you time to do what you want! Sign-up and join today—it's free—and sign up your friends and family, too! It's easy the Semi-Homemade way! Visit the site today and start enjoying your busy life!

Sign yourself and your friends and family up to the semi-homemaker's club today!

About Sandra Lee

Sandra Lee is a *New York Times* best-selling autho and a nationally acclaimed lifestyle expert. He signature Semi-Homemade approach to cookin home decorating, gardening, crafting, entertainin beauty, and fashion offers savvy shortcuts an down-to-earth secrets for creating a beautifu affordable, and most importantly doable lifestyle.

Sandra Lee's cookbook series offers amazing meal in minutes, fabulous food fixin's, and sensational— yet simple—style ideas. *Semi-Homemade Cookin with Sandra Lee* is one of Food Network's hottes cooking shows, providing many helpful hint timesaving techniques, tips, and tricks.

Find even more sensible, savvy solutions online a **semihomemade.com**.